Under His
SHADOW

Based on a True Story

DEBRA MARTINEZ

ISBN 979-8-89130-659-2 (paperback)
ISBN 979-8-89345-166-5 (hardcover)
ISBN 979-8-89130-660-8 (digital)

Christian Faith Publishing
832 Park Avenue
Meadville, PA 16335
www.christianfaithpublishing.com

Printed in the United States of America

Have you ever felt like there must be more than just fulfilling responsibility and working? Is there any hope of balancing motherhood, marriage, and running a business? Balancing motherhood, marriage, and running a business can be challenging, but is that all there is to who I am? It is hard being a mother, wife, and business owner. Is that all there is of me? Can there be something else to bring comfort and fulfillment to your life? If there was it would come unexpectedly, and I see myself in a dark place and my world crashing down. As I stayed caring for Mark through his illness and then watching Israel battling through Hodgkins Lyonhoma; leaving my heart would be broken. It has taken me many years to get through the pain and suffering. It felt strange to know one day, my long-endured grief will bring joy back to my life, and I'll be seeing my life on to another journey in life that I knew little to nothing about to another location and another address. It would be there when everything would make sense, and I'll find peace and joy, leaving one question on my mind: Why and for how long? It would be years later. And while I was writing my manuscript, something happened, and I'd see myself admitted to the hospital. No sooner after being admitted, the day after that, I'd be awakened, hearing two men were speaking. At that moment, I could not see anyone else around. But, only heard them talking as I stared at where the voices were coming from, leaving my heart racing, thinking about what to do next when I suddenly whispered hello. After whispering, my hospital room became quiet, and the only sounds I would hear next would be the pounding of my heart as fear settled within me, making it harder to fathom if this was happening. The whole scene felt like something out of a scary movie. And there I was, frightened, paralyzed, wondering what would happen next. It wasn't long, as I kept staring at where the voices were coming from, that I whispered another hello, leaving me spooked, as I closed my eyes, trying to forget what was happening.

It wouldn't be long after I fell back to sleep that I'd be awakened again, this time by a kick and rattling ticking sounds, causing me to jump. They're, e reaching for the call nurse button; I'd be in a panic, hearing a woman's voice asking her to hurry; something strange was happening in my room. When the lights in my room came on, I would see two nurses coming toward me as they began pressing on the control panel, trying to get the noises to stop. That moment looked crazy as the nurses pressed the buttons, making the ticking sounds stop.

When the woman nurse realized what they were doing wasn't working, she stopped and asked the male nurses to go around and unplug the power cord from the wall. After several attempts, she noticed it wouldn't work and told the male nurse to drop the power cord as she reevaluated my care plan. Although my story wasn't over, the bizarre things I'd be experiencing would keep me remembering the good things that would appear to rescue me from my deepest emotions. Interestingly, unaware of what more was going to happen, a day would come when it would finally make sense that my life would be so much more extraordinary and would be rewritten.

Beginning

I was eighteen years old when Israel and I were married. Shortly after marriage, I gave birth to our first son, Israel III, before Israel nicknamed him Coco. It was during my first weeks after giving birth that Israel returned to work, serving in the United States Army at Fort Sam Houston, while I remained home, caring for our son.

*****

Although having my firstborn child is a gift, it wouldn't be long after giving birth that I became depressed; I'm not sure why or what made me feel this way. When Israel received orders from the Defense Department a year later, we were leaving San Antonio for a different lifestyle that I wouldn't be accustomed to in a small town away from an army military institution in a town called McAllen, Texas. Being a daughter of a serviceman in World War II retired in the United States Army, somehow I knew this assignment would be different, and service and duty would be part of the package.

When the time came for Israel and I to relocate to McAllen, I'd be saddened to say goodbye to my mother and my siblings as I prepared for my next move alongside Israel to his next military assignment. Although being married to a man in uniform as he served his country, there would come a time when I saw my life not as easy and finding myself alone.

It is noticeable that if I were married to a police officer, his assigned duties and careers would be risky. How about firemen? They also take risks, and what are the chances of a roof collapsing, hurting, or getting killed? Whatever career Israel chose, one thing was that a spouse's life in these careers would be similar in serving our state and country.

When the day came, we relocated to McAllen. I would be excited and ready for Israel's next assignment and be supporting him along the way. On that day of the move, we would be arriving in Rio Grande Valley. On that day, Israel would have an apartment ready for Coco and me and receive our household goods later that week. After everything was put away. There would be days when my excitement faded. Leaving me lonely.

During that time, Israel worked late hours. While Coco and I were settling into the apartment, I'll be feeling vulnerable, missing my family, and unsure about what I should do there and the direction to go. At that moment, I began to wonder if I should walk away before considering the effect it would have on Coco being away from his father.

The challenges I faced in McAllen many weeks later came with limitations. First, if I wanted to work, I would need a car, but I had to learn how to drive. If I found employment, I would need childcare. While all of these things revolved in my mind, one thing is for sure: It would be impossible not knowing how to drive and trusting someone to care for my child.

In the following weeks, I would have a routine that remained the same: It was just Coco and me, while Israel continued working late. The only options I had left would be caring for Coco and watching television until one afternoon, when I heard children laughing outside the window.

Looking out the window, I saw children playing in the pool, so I hurried to get Coco into his swimwear. It wouldn't be long after arriving two women greeted me and introduced themselves. As we chatted, their children came over and began playing with Coco. The first woman was an American Indian from Oklahoma with two little girls; the other woman was a widower with two sons attending high school, and a daughter named Emily. After spending my day with them, it wasn't long before sundown arrived that I was asked where I was living, and I was pointing to the apartment from the pool.

Once I returned to the apartment, I began getting Coco ready for bed. After his bath, I lay Coco in bed and fell asleep while waiting for Israel. When I heard the front door open, I saw Israel arriving home in the wee morning hour, asking where he'd been and was told, "Having a few drinks with the guys from the battalion." However, the time was nearly four in the morning. I was feeling bothered about why he didn't call home.

Later that morning, I met up with my friend and began to feel better about my move to McAllen. The thought of having someone around to chat with would make my time in McAllen a little easier. The days living there did linger, and my nights after Coco was asleep left me lonely, even though I was willing to hold on to this significant change. At the same time, Israel served as a United States recruiter in McAllen. It wouldn't be long before I was battling anorexia and bulimia, finding it hard to break away. The small steps that spiral out of control would trap me, and the next is, I'd be seeing a way to survive, even though, at that time, I had nothing to gain but a lot to lose.

What I can say is, puking somehow made me feel better. The more weight I lost, the thinner and thinner I got. Exercising and puking became my relief. But while I watched my health spiral down a dark tunnel, there wasn't anything I could do to control the hurt and pain I was feeling. The more of not having Israel around made it more difficult, leaving me to wonder if it was me. My wight went from 225 pounds to 105 in less than eleven months. I wouldn't know how to escape from it as I looked in the mirror, wondering how long I would survive, unsure and not having an explanation for why I was doing this to myself as the disease shadowed my life.

As much as I was going through times of being lonely. A day came when I called Israel and explained that I had awakened from passing out. After telling him this, he rushed home and took me to the emergency room, where I lay lying on a gurney, hooked up to fluids, while the doctors waited for my lab results. It would be late when I was discharged and placed on bed rest.

The following morning, I awoke and saw Israel home caring for Coco. That week, when I got my strength back, Israel returned to work, and I was back on the bathroom floor in tears. Days later, when I felt better, I took Coco to the pool and saw my friends there. One of them said, "Missed you." Hearing what she said left me smiling, thinking how good it felt to know you were missed.

A few days later, Emily's mom asked, "If you are interested in working, don't worry. I can take care of Coco." After hearing her, my heart raced, knowing that was what I needed to keep me busy, and it wouldn't be long before I considered her offer and our friendship grew, and she became like another mother to me. Shortly after being hired, I worked at a Chinese Restaurant at the corner of Nolan Loop. After working there for several weeks, it wasn't long before, I started feeling excited about how the owners were treating me, making me part of their family.

After working months for them, I was in the kitchen, holding a wok to cook a customer's order for a drive-through. Grabbing that huge wok and flipping the vegetables up and over was something I had always seen the owner's husband do many times. And there I was, ecstatic that I could take care of customers while the owner was in the middle of their argument.

The months I spent working at working in China North was an honor. There were so many memories that I still remember; however, there is one that I wouldn't forget. I was sitting with the owner's wife, and we were rolling dinner napkins when she asked me to select something from the menu for me to eat. I explained to her that I had never eaten Chinese food, and after telling her that, she rose and went to the kitchen, leaving me alone. At the same time, I was rolling napkins. It didn't take long before I saw her husband carrying a serving tray filled with different cuisines, while she carried the two bowls of steamed rice, smiling, placing the two-rice bowls on the table before grabbing a pair of chopsticks, still smiling, and said eat, "There."

I stared at the cuisine she had her husband cook, smiling, picking up the other bowl of rice, and adding soy sauce before saying, "Thank you. This is perfect." That was my first time eating soy sauce. It didn't take long after hearing the owner say "you need to eat and gain weight" that she continued asking her husband to cook meals for us and for me to taste before vegetable fried rice became my favorite dish, and the owner insisted that I eat and gain some weight. Shortly after the months working there in the winter, I got pregnant again, and they were worried about me slipping. When they handed me a document to sign, I looked at them while they stared at me; it wouldn't be long when I said "I won't sue if I fell," and left it unsigned as they smiled, hearing her husband say, "I don't want to see you in the kitchen cooking or getting the dinner plates. I will bring them to you." At that moment, I saw the relief in their eyes and felt excited that they didn't let me go.

On the day of my OBGYN appointment, I was told I was just a few weeks pregnant. After hearing the news that day, all I did was think about the weight I would gain, which frightened me. But somehow I knew I had to get passed my fear and remember I was carrying a new life inside me.

In December 1990, Israel planned a trip for us to Puerto Rico to visit his family, which left me excited. The thought of going to Puerto Rico for Christmas was something we both needed. So when that day came, we arrived in San Antonio the night before our flight, and I was looking forward to my trip.

Our flight from San Antonio to San Juan would be long, even though we would arrive there in San Juan later in the evening. When we finally reached Israel's grandmother's house, Israel pulled up on the driveway. We heard music playing and the strings of a guitar when we were greeted by his family members and served food. It wouldn't be long before the music got serious when I heard Israel's little brother singing and saw his father playing an instrument, welcoming us there. But then, while his brother sang, Israel jumped in to sing, and we all clapped and sang to the beat of the rhythm until the wee morning hours, and by then, I was exhausted and looking for a place to lay my head. Shortly after, his aunt showed me where I could rest; it didn't take long before I heard Israel say, "Let's go," and we were driving up a mountain to his parent's home.

Driving up the mountain wasn't something I enjoyed. There were times that I thought the car could flip backward after going up that steep hill. But as frightened as I was, I'd battled my fears as I held my breath and closed my eyes, counting all the way up until I felt the car tires resting on the flat surface.

In the days that followed at San German, a day came when Israel and his father began preparing to slaughter a pig to roast for the family Christmas gathering. It was a tradition every year that a pig would be killed and served for their Christmas dinner. At that time, and that day, it would be held at his mother and father's house.

At the same time, Israel's family members were arriving. The music were playing, and I was helping my sister-in-law pass out finger foods and crackers as I watched Israel sharpening a machete and two knives. It wouldn't be long before Israel brought up my pregnancy to his father and aunt. There, he and his aunt went back and forth, joking and calling him a liar in Spanish. It looked hilarious as he kept repeatedly telling her the same thing when she turned to me, saying in Spanish, "Yuyo is lying." Smiling, I looked at Israel and confirmed to them that I was pregnant, and suddenly, everything they were doing stopped, and we were congratulated with hugs and kisses. Once that was over, it didn't take long before I heard an awful squealing sound, making me sick and want to lie down.

Finally, the pig was killed, roasted, and cooked when Israel's relatives began to leave. After returning to my room, my in-laws were excited knowing that another child was on the way and knowing it was my birthday. We all met at his grandmother's home the following day to celebrate Christmas, New Year, and Three Kings' Day, after enjoying the parties and gatherings, the day came when we had to return to McAllen.

On the day of our flight out from San Juan, we are crying, saying our goodbyes. Seeing his family in tears affected me emotionally. I didn't want to see them upset or leave them in tears. And after seeing their love for me, I felt lucky to have in-laws and his siblings loving me as one of their daughters and sister.

Today I can still sense the feeling of love that they showed me, remembering the Christmas tree that lit up the mountaintop as we waved goodbye from the car window as we drove down the mountain, taking with us the tears that we wiped from our eyes as they stood standing as the car drifted away.

When we arrived at the airport in San Juan, we boarded the plane and were seated in the middle. Shortly after takeoff, it didn't take long before we were in the air when we saw the captain and another crew member exiting the cockpit and walking toward the back of the aircraft. Unsure of the reason why, I remained seated, even though I was curious as I played with Coco, staying optimistic, reminding myself that nothing was wrong as we flew over the Atlantic Ocean.

When the captain returned to the cockpit with his crew member, *it* didn't take long before he exited the cockpit again with another crew member, carrying a screwdriver. At that moment, I leaned over to Israel, saying something was wrong with the plane before he began to shoo me. Whatever the captain was doing in the back of the aircraft was a cause for concern. It was not like he needed to fix a coffee maker or screw something loose from an appliance. But whatever it was, when the captain returned to the cockpit, we would hear his voice, asking us to remain seated with our seat belts fastened and refrain from standing or using the restroom.

It wasn't long before the crew members began passing out handsets and peanuts and offered cold drinks as the movie played for us to watch. Later, as we watched the film, we heard the captain's voice on the intercom, telling his crew to prepare for landing. Once the aircraft landed, the captain returned to speaking, informing all the passengers to remain seated. We were unsure why. We were sitting in the plane for so long that my headache worsened before I approached one of the stewards, asking for a headache medicine.

When she handed me a cup of water and pills, I shared with her that I was a few weeks pregnant and needed fresh air. After listening to my concerns, she advised me to return to my seat and wait while informing the captain. It wouldn't be long when the stewards returned, saying that the captain ordered the doors to be opened. Once the doors were opened, I needed to remain at the terminal. After agreeing with her, it wasn't long before the doors opened, and I exited the cabin and walked around.

As I walked through the airport, I ran into a Mickey and Minnie Mouse display, wondering where we were. There, feeling concerned about our next flight out from Dallas, I hurried to ask one of the airport employees where I was then smiled upon hearing that I was in Fort Lauderdale, Florida, reacting as I rushed back to the airplane to inform Israel.

At the same time I was telling Israel this, the two women across from us arose, grabbed their things, and exited the cabin, and it wasn't long before the rest of the passengers followed. When Israel and I took Coco off the plane, I waited while Israel stood in line with the other passengers. There, I'd see the airline's mechanic, working on the engines. I knew something was wrong but was thankful nothing horrible happened to all of us after noticing the terminal sign stating closed. It didn't take long before I heard Israel say, "Let's hurry. The aircraft is waiting for us."

When we arrived and entered the flight, I caught sight of the passenger's faces as the stewardess placed us in first class, unaware that our flight would be flying straight to San

Antonio. When we arrived in San Antonio, it took many hours later when we came home in the wee morning hours. The following day, Israel returned to work, and I was getting ready for my first real appointment at my OBGYN office.

Unfortunately, visiting the OBGYN wouldn't be one of my favorite places; however, I knew how critical the care of my first trimester was before hearing the doctor's input. He considered that I needed to gain weight and eat for two. Hearing his concern left me in tears, feeling my secrets were exposed but smiling, trying to make myself feel better.

Once I left the doctor's office, I picked up Coco and told Emily's mother what the doctor had told me and what he expected me to do. You should've seen the look on her face when I told her I was battling bulimia and anorexia. Although this would be the first time telling anyone, at that moment, I felt as if she already knew but never brought it up when we were together.

The thoughts and concerns of gaining pounds would haunt me. However, what could I do? There were times that I'd be forcing myself to eat, even though I wouldn't gain the weight the doctor expected.

On August 1, 1991, my water broke while watching a talk show, then I called Emily's mother for help. When she arrived at the apartment, I see her sons and little Emily. She noticed I hadn't changed my clothes as I hurried to get cleaned up after returning to the living room. I heard her say to her sons, "Drive her to the hospital while I watched Coco and Emily." Once I arrived at their car, it would be Emily's older brother that would be driving me to the hospital. When I heard his blinkers blinking, I seated in the back seat with his younger brother, laughing as his older brother honked the car horn to the hospital.

After arriving at the hospital, I was admitted and placed in one of the labor rooms and hooked to a baby monitor. It didn't take long before I was in pain, and I was asking the nurse where the doctor was and was told he would be here soon. The few hours in labor felt like an eternity as my contractions increased, and it wasn't long before I asked again where my doctor was. It didn't take long after speaking to the nurse that I would see an anesthesiologist enter the room and give me an epidural. And just like that, my pain went away. Shortly after that, my doctor arrived. Next, I heard, "Get her into the operating room now." And just like that, after placing a metallic hat on my head, the only noise I heard was my baby crying, and my doctor congratulating me that I had a baby boy as I dozed off.

It would be later in the afternoon when I awakened and saw a nurse sitting beside me there, having difficulty speaking. I was trying to ask for a cup of water when she came by me and removed the oxygen mask, and I repeated myself for a cup of water. When the nurse returned, she was smiling.

"Someone here to see you."

When I saw who it was, I was excited to see Emily's mother and heard she her speaking to Israel, and he said he would be home tomorrow. Suddenly, my heart dropped, worrying about Coco. While Emily's mom and I were chatting, I heard the nurse say, "You have more visitors here to see you." I smiled as they came walking in. They were the friends and coworkers from the recruiting battalion where Israel worked that came to see the baby and updated me about Israel returning home in the morning. Hearing what I already knew would leave me vulnerable. Although thinking about a new life that I brought into this world left me scared, at the same time, my insecurities left me vulnerable while I hid my sadness from my eyes.

Several minutes later, I was talking with his coworkers when Emily's mother pulled out a picture of my baby that was taken right after his birth. We looked at the photo as she explained why she had taken the picture. Her story was, "Haven't you seen the news about babies being switched at birth and stolen from nurseries?" The thought of something like that happening was rare. However, I was grateful to have her as my friend.

The time we stood there, we were laughing, knowing it sounded ridiculous, even though it was true. You couldn't imagine that in the year 1991, the things happening in hospitals and maternity wards would be one thing I'd be worried about. However, seeing the photo of my baby and having Emily's mom beside me brought tranquility. Once Israel's coworkers left, it didn't take long before Emily's mom said her goodbye, and I was alone.

As I remained in the recovery room alone, I considered the following plan for my life with another child. Would I continue to work? What would be my next move? Would there be challenges I would face again? At the same time, the questions settled within me. One thing would be true, no matter how deep they were, I knew I would have to face them somehow. While I was alone, the nurse brought another new mother to the recovery room, and we chatted.

She had just given birth to a girl and didn't have a name picked out for her as she had planned. She was sure she be having another boy. While I stared at her holding her baby, it would be long when she asked me if I gave birth to a boy or a girl. I answered a boy. After chatting, I asked her if she had a name selected for her son before she found out she had given birth to a girl. She answered she was planning to name him

Mark and now had to think about a girl's name for the baby. As I thought about the name Mark, it didn't take long before I joined Israel's middle name, Anthony, then I realized it was perfect. That evening, my baby would be given a name.

*****

Later in the evening, after I named my child Mark, the woman next to me was discharged, and I was alone again.

At the same time, the nurses came in and out of the recovery room. It wouldn't be long before I stopped one of them, asking when I would be transported to the maternity room to be with my baby. After answering and being told she didn't know, I was informed that the hospital delivered too many deliveries that day, leaving the nursery over its capacity, and that they were placing new mothers on different floors with their babies. Still they found it challenging to find a place for me.

As time passed, it the nurses brought Mark to me, and I was holding him for the first time. Although I wouldn't have Mark for long, the little time I held him would make me feel better.

Once Mark returned to the nursery, I stopped one of the nurses and asked why it was taking them too long to move me. After hearing there weren't more rooms available except for VIP suites in the maternity ward, I got upset, asking, "Please call my medical insurance company and move to one of those VIP rooms," unsure where I would be sleeping tonight.

Shortly after the nurse left, another nurse arrived and said my private suite was ready. When I arrived in my room, I was upset, crying about what was happening around me. I was missing my son Coco and thinking about what was next.

If I was going to get through the challenges of my past, how would I get through the challenges right now? If only I knew what the price would come later in life would cost me.

The following morning, when Israel arrived at the hospital with Coco, they would get to see and be holding the baby in their arms. It wouldn't be long while Israel had Mark in his arms when he heard Mark's name for the first time. There he got up, leaned over, and kissed me before saying he was leaving, saying he would get lunch for Coco before he would fall asleep.

When they had left, I'd be alone with Mark before a nurse returned, taking Mark back to the nursery. The way I felt at that moment would be indescribable, and why I felt this way would be unknown if it were just baby blues or fear. Who knows? However, whatever it was, somehow I learned that I would have a long road ahead.

Days later, after being discharged from the hospital, it wouldn't be long after coming home that I returned to San Antonio for a few months and worked while their grandparents watched the boys. It wasn't long before Israel returned to San Antonio to attend the district area recruiter conference that Sunday afternoon that I chose to return to McAllen that Sunday evening. When we arrived back home, I entered and saw my things moved. It was until the next day that afternoon that I caught Israel having an affair. There the woman asked on the phone who I was, and where had been before telling her I was having his baby. That was life in the military. My father cheated, and now I would learn that my husband did too.

After confronting Israel, I wasn't the one that needed to choose, and I wasn't going to be the person to make it right. He did this and needed to be the one to correct it. After the woman called again, I handed him the phone while I watched him end it. There I became strong, staring at him knowing what he had done to me, left me heartbroken and I wanted the pain to disappear. Why did he do it? No matter how I felt then, Israel would do his best to make me feel better, to the point of sending me to driver Ed to learn how to drive.

During that time, I would hear about many more of his affairs, trying to make our marriage work. In the following months, I felt like I was the oldest woman behind the wheels in the driver's seat while the teenagers remained sitting and waiting for their turn to drive. When the instructor smiled and said, "Next time, bring pillows to sit on it," I took it as a joke, especially when he said after I was too old to learn to drive. It wouldn't be long before I received my driver's license, and Israel surprised me with a new car. Even though I was doing my best to trust him, it would be long before military orders arrived.

As we continued working on our marriage, it wouldn't be long before Israel received orders overseas to Camp Casey, Korea, and the boys and I would be living back in San Antonio. When we found an apartment, the boys and I lived near the military base, and I worked before seeing myself out with friends and leaving my sons with a babysitter. It would be months later that I would confess to an affair. Even though I came clean and told Israel about the matter, our marriage didn't crumble. When Israel completed his one-year tour in Korea, he returned to his old duty station at Fort Sam Houston just before closing on our new home.

While I continued working, Israel would be on leave and be moving things to our new home. By the weekend, I'd take the weekend off and assist Israel with whatever needed to be moved. The few months living in our new home were fantastic. Coco will be six years old, and Mark will be past his first year old.

After a few months of living in our new home with my boys, there would be many memories I could still recollect. However, there is one that I couldn't stop thinking about, and I wouldn't share it with anyone.

It was springtime one late afternoon. Mark was a thin and small child, always barefoot but gentle and the cutest, caring little boy. He was always happy, smiling, and always taking off his shoes and clothing, and seeing him only in diaper. Sometimes I wonder if he was allergic to clothing. The best part of Mark running around without clothes is that Mark didn't wear his clothes long enough to get dirty. All the times I chased him to get his shoes and clothes back on, the faster he would be in getting them off. However, he was just sixteen months old, and something unique about him felt different.

It was late one weekend afternoon that I told Israel I needed to go to the grocery store and asked him where the boys were. There he said they were upstairs, Coco was playing video games, and Mark was asleep. It seemed just the right time to leave while Israel cared for them while I went to the store. However, when I arrived at the grocery store, I parked my car and pulled the driver's seat forward, reached for my purse, grabbed hold of my work jacket, and saw a little body staring at me with his gooey eyes and a huge smile, finding Mark there.

In a quick response, I asked him how he got into the car and only heard his gibberish speech as I picked him up and carried him to the store with me.

After rushing to get what I needed from the store, I returned home, parked my car in the garage, and stood in the hallway, calling out to Israel. When Israel answered, I asked where the boys were and again heard they were upstairs. There hurrying to surprise him as I stormed into the kitchen, asking, "Who is this?" As I saw Israel's mouth was wide open before asking where I found him. Bravely, I responded, "Sitting on the floor of the driver's side under my work coat."

*****

That was the last time I ever asked Israel the whereabouts of our boys. From then on, I wouldn't leave the house without checking the vehicle first. Though that incident was so many years ago, one thing that still makes me wonder is how Mark was able to open and close the door, being sixteen months old. At that age, it would've been impossible for him to do so. Nevertheless, a day would come when Mark would get older when that story would come to my memory, and I would see my life shattered, lying on my bed, grabbing my pillow, crying, not knowing why this was happening!

A few years later, Israel's military life would separate us again. Israel would be returning to another overseas assignment in Korea. Though I knew service and duty were part of his career, while Israel completed his second tour in Korea and received another set of orders, he would be stationed at another duty station at Fort Lewis, Washington. At the same time, the boys and I remained living in Texas.

By fall, Israel was settling at his new duty station in Fort Lewis. I resigned from my employment, unsure what to do with my time alone while our boys were at school. It wouldn't be long before my ex-boss asked for a favor to babysit her kids at her house. After agreeing, I spent part of the morning caring for them and had much fun. When the girl's mother returned home that afternoon, she saw that the girls were napping, and I stayed there chatting.

It wasn't long before she began talking about her girl's home day care and trying to convince me I should apply. It left me laughing, imagining what my home would look like. But after listening to her suggestion, I told her I would think about it.

It would be a few weeks when I thought of opening childcare in my home. And after researching it and filling out the application, it wasn't long before my house became certified as a registered family home. A year later, during my first inspection, I was told that I was overqualified as a registered family home and asked if I would be interested in becoming a licensed group home.

Upon hearing my options, it wasn't long before my licensing representative made it easy. She mailed the applications, and I became a licensed family group home within two months. Shortly after becoming licensed, it wouldn't be long before I would see my success printed in the city's local San Antonio Light business column. Somehow, I became a successful businesswoman, wife, and mother. The thoughts of me carrying part of my life as an American soldier's wife—I never regretted it.

However, Israel and I had to sacrifice some choices of us being together. We knew we didn't want to see our sons go back and forth with different schools and have friends scattered around the world. The years of being home and providing childcare kept me busy, and being home with our boys made my life more accessible for emergencies. However, a day would come when everything that was keeping me together while Israel was away, serving this county, would begin to tumble down, leaving me in grief, thinking of a way out of my misery, fighting the situation head-on, even though it was out of my hands.

How could anyone handle a situation they have no control over? What would be my results if I gave up and walked away? What would drive you to get past your emotional state of fear? Although many questions were floating in my mind. The whole point of thinking about them leads me to test my strength.

It was the beginning of 2004, a year I waited so long to arrive. When springtime approached, people would be prepping their gardens or cleaning up their garages or homes, eliminating the clutter. But as for me, my mind was thankful and excited, preparing for the homecoming of Israel's retirement. So while I was waiting for the good news of Israel returning home and retiring, I'd be getting our home back to what it was, painting the walls, and eliminating the clutter I accumulated through the years as I continued operating my business and caring for our boys, who were now in their teenage years.

Weeks turned into months. It was at the end of summer when I heard Israel's exciting news, saying, "Honey, I'm retiring and coming home." Hearing his words left me confused, not expecting the time to come so quickly. Nevertheless, I was still be excited that Israel was finally coming home, and we were reuniting as a family. However, if I thought Israel would be returning home quicker, who would have known that while I was preparing a welcome-home reception, the Defense Department had something else in mind.

Later that evening, after hanging up the telephone, I was thinking about what I should do about my business. I knew it would be hard for Israel to be home and rest with many children running around. Somehow, I had to figure out a plan before Israel's retirement.

In the following weeks, I didn't hear Israel mention anything more about his retirement as days turned into weeks. It wouldn't be long before I asked when he would be retiring and would have nothing to say about it. But if he was withholding something from me, it wouldn't be long. Whatever he was withholding from me would be exposed, and I'd be hearing a whole different story.

It was one Friday evening, around the same time Israel would call home. I was up that night, while the boys were already in their room, playing their video games, when I heard the telephone ring. When I answered the telephone, Israel was speaking in a low tone. I asked him to speak up. Suddenly I heard him say out loud, "There's not going to be a retirement, and I have orders waiting at another military base in Fort Stewart, Georgia."

At that moment, I felt everything I held together was coming apart. I always supported Israel and his career while he'd been serving this country for many years, but this time it left me powerless about what to say next. It didn't take long before I got the urge to speak up, asking, "What do you mean you have orders to another base?" "Look, you promised to come home after completing the remainder of your enlistment." But unfortunately, after a few minutes of speaking to Israel, I couldn't keep hearing what more he had to say. I was broken and wanted him home, thinking how much time our boys lost not having their father home and hearing his words that never failed, "I'm only doing this for you and the boys to have everything." If that was true, one thing is for sure: He would miss seeing our sons growing into caring young men, while he continued to serve this great nation.

When the sun rose the following day, I'd be awakened, preparing breakfast for my boys before they came down to eat. It wouldn't be long after they had eaten and left for school that I began to weep. Suddenly, I would see the front door open. My student started to walk in for breakfast. After serving the children breakfast, my assistant arrived and noticed I had been crying, asking, "What happened?" After crying more, I began wiping off my tears, telling her about Israel, that he wasn't returning home anytime soon, and orders were waiting for him at another duty base in Fort Stewart, Georgia. After she had heard what was happening, she got up and said, "Girl, you had me worried for a moment," causing me to laugh. "Well, at least we don't have to search for boxes." I laughed as tears flowed from my eyes.

The thought of what she said made sense. I didn't have to go looking for boxes needed, to be worried about finding another place to relocate my business. Whatever was going to happen, one thing was for sure: Our boys would be with me and in school while my business rose in success.

I returned to the classroom and started my day with my assistant and our children.

The day went by fast, and all the children had be gone by the time I knew it. Later that night, I called Israel to get more information about his orders but was told he didn't know much about his assignment. When December arrived, Israel made plans for Mark and me to visit him in Tacoma before departing to his next duty station.

On the day of departure from San Antonio, Coco drove us to the airport, leaving him one rule to follow—be careful driving to and from your auntie's house and going to work—before kissing him goodbye. When Mark and I boarded the plane, we comfortably buckled up while I watched Mark place his headset to listen to music.

The flight to Seattle would be nonstop. When we arrived in Seattle, Israel was waiting, smiling, leading us out of the airport and to his car. Finally, when we arrived at Israel's apartment and entered, I smelled his famous Puerto Rican rice before going to Israel's room to nap. Hours later, I awakened to see Mark sitting on one of his twin beds, still holding his game, while Israel played a crossword puzzle.

When Israel saw that I had awakened, he hurried to the kitchen to warm up the food he had cooked hours earlier. Then, after placing a movie in his DVR for us to watch, a few hours later, I returned to bed after showering, while Israel remained in the living room with Mark.

Early the following morning, I was awakened by noises and saw Israel dressed in his BDU. There he asked me to get up and look out the window. After doing so, I opened the blinds and saw the backyard covered in snow, thinking about our arrival yesterday in warm and sunny weather, now seeing it covered in snow. I was unsure how many warm outfits Mark and I had in our luggage as I stayed looking at the branches that I heard had cracked before they fell.

Long after my eyes stayed glued, the snow took me back to my childhood memories of living in Frankfurt, Germany. I'd be skating in my socks with my sisters before running inside the house to get warm by the furnace in the basement.

I didn't know what drew me to remember my childhood memories. Although there were some I did want to remember again. However, the ones I didn't want to remember wouldn't affect me as they should have, although I had a life different than my siblings', one thing was for sure: When Mom and my brother and I were homeless, I never forgot what it was like to have nothing. And, yes, whatever I didn't have as a child prepared me for life and something more significant that led me on being grateful for what I am and what I had accomplished in life.

As I continuously looked out the window, I heard more branches breaking, thinking about how nice it would be to sip on a cup of hot chocolate over vanilla ice cream. Standing at the window for a little longer, I turned and saw Israel coming out of the bathroom, smelling his cologne. After he kissed me, he said an extra set of keys were hanging in the kitchen if I wanted to go out. Once I heard the front door locked, I checked on Mark, noticed he was asleep, and returned to bed.

Later that afternoon, I saw Mark playing games. I asked him to get dressed. Once dressed, we left the apartment and searched for the nearest convenience store to buy a pint of ice cream and a cup of hot chocolate. Unsure which way to go, we went right, walking three blocks, and came across the closest convenience store. Once we entered, we were greeted by an Asian man with an enormous smile. I asked if he had any pints of vanilla ice cream to sell. Smiling, he answered yes, turning around to bring one.

While the Asian left us alone, I saw Mark pulling snacks off the shelves, while my eyes caught sight of a hot chocolate machine. I raced to pour myself a cup. After filling my cup, I heard Mark's voice calling out, "Mom, Mom." Turning around, I saw Mark's arms filled with snacks, asking him to put the items on the countertop.

When the Asian man returned with an enormous smile, he asked if I needed anything more as he glanced out the window, noticing the weather worsening, smiling back at me.

After he had totaled it all up, I paid him and closed the door, making our way back to the apartment. When Mark and I arrived at the apartment's parking lot, Mark began playing in the snow. I realized this was the first time, so I took snapshots of Mark playing in the snow.

After taking snapshots of Mark, I thought about Coco and wondered what he was doing. I wondered why this trip happened this way, though it would make sense later. If this trip had a purpose, it would come back and haunt me, and I would learn that I would have no power over it.

Mark and I stood in the snow. We were both cold and wet. Finally, we rushed back into the apartment to remove our clothes and placed our wet clothes to wash.

When I saw the front door opened after returning, I saw Israel coming home from work. There, he told me he had week off, and Washington was under an arctic winter blast going to lockdown. It left me blown away by how fast the weather changed from yesterday.

While Israel stayed focused on his crossword puzzles, Mark would be in tune with his games and me. While I was in the kitchen, cooking stews and meals, I watched the snowflakes fall from the window.

When the day came for Mark and I to return to San Antonio, we will arrive at Seattle airport and be told our flights were canceled, leaving me worried. Finally, three days later, Mark and I arrived home in San Antonio and saw Coco waiting to bring us home. When we came home, we rushed into the house, leaving our luggage at the door, and hurried to bed.

In the morning, I was the first to awake and sitting in the classroom, looking over the schedule for the week, then I heard footsteps upstairs.

After getting up, I went to the kitchen to prepare breakfast for my boys before making breakfast for my students. When Mark and Coco came down, I saw how exhausted they were as they grabbed their breakfast and kissed me goodbye before closing the door behind them.

The next time I saw the door opened again, I heard a little voice, yelling, "Miss Debbie, Miss Debbie." The boy ran to me and hugged me.

There I looked at his little face and saw his hazel eyes, noticing how excited he was to return to school, warming my heart. So, after serving him and the other children breakfast,

I changed the program that day, making it memorable for the children, naming the theme "Winter Wonderland in the Seventies." Then, when my assistant arrived, I briefed her as that music was playing, handing her paper plates to pass out to the children so they could slide around the house.

Shortly after skating around the house, we gave the children a piece of paper and asked them to crumble it, making snowballs before throwing them at each other. Unfortunately, it didn't be long after tossing the snowballs when one of the children grabbed the beanbags and threw them at us, striking me in the face and causing me to yell, "Freeze," asking the children to hand them over.

As I looked at what time it was, I realized it was close to lunch time. I asked my assistant to take the children to recess. Once all the children's coats and jackets were on, they were excited to hear that they were going outside to play with the commercial playground equipment they have in the playground. After the kitchen door closed, I thought about what to cook. I grab the phonebook and ordered pizza and ran to the store to get chips, carrots, and ice cream, unaware that the children were hiding candies in their pockets.

After making lunch plates, I asked my assistant to bring the children back inside and let them wash their hands and faces before they sit to eat. Unfortunately, after they were seated, some of the children began to fall asleep while they were eating, and we hurried back to the classroom to clean it up before placing their mats on the floor.

When we arrived back in the kitchen, most of the children were asleep, and we carried them to the classroom, laying them on the mat and covering them up as the soothing music played.

Shortly after returning to the kitchen and cleaning, we laughed when we saw gums and candies that the children chewed spitted on the floor. We scraped them off. I was still laughing when I said, "I don't want ever to see a piece of gum or candy." That afternoon, when the children had gone home, I was excited to be home, and everything was returning to normal. However, one thing was for sure: When Israel arrived at his next duty station, I was shocked at what I'd heard.

On the day of Israel's move, it was June when the movers came knocking. That morning, Israel called home early to inform me that he had everything he needed packed and placed in the car.

While we were talking when, Israel heard a knock on the door and told me, "I'll call you back." Hours later, Israel called home, letting me know that the apartment was empty, and he was going to a hotel to rest. After hanging up, I returned to the classroom and waited for the children to go home, trying not to think about Israel's assignment.

After picking up dinner for the boys, I showered and got ready for bed, finding it difficult to sleep. There I kept tossing and turning before staring at the clock.

The thoughts of Israel's assignment being so secret concerned me. Israel was nearly twenty years in serving in the United States Army and knew he wasn't far from retirement. As I lay in bed, the time was nearly five o'clock in the morning. It wouldn't be long before the telephone rang, and I heard Israel's voice, informing me he was leaving Fort Lewis, Washington, to make his way to his next duty station in Fort Stewart, Georgia. Then I told him to drive safely and not to drive at a high speed, kissing him over the phone. That was the last time I heard from him until he reached the grounds of Fort Stewart, Georgia.

It took Israel several days until he arrived at Fort Stewart, Georgia, and when he did, it was right at sundown when he settled in a hotel room at the Travelodge at Fort Stewart.

Once Israel had taken all of his things out of the car, he called home, telling me he had made it safely and would step out for a while to get something to eat.

After hanging up, I returned to the classroom to prepare my students for recess while my assistant cleaned up. But as I thought of what Israel would be assigned and ordered to do, I didn't allow my feeling to show, knowing that the Defense Department of the United States Army had given him a special assignment.

Later that evening, while our sons were getting ready for bed, I went to my room and lay on the bed before showering. After showering, it was another difficult night to sleep. I stared at the clock many hours later, thinking I had three more hours left before it was time to wake up.

It wouldn't be long before I heard the telephone ring, hearing Israel's voice on the other end. He informed me that he was leaving the room to eat breakfast before going to base headquarters to get briefed about his assignment. It was not long before I kissed him over the phone, saying, "I love you. I'll call you later."

After we hang up, I arose from bed and made a cup of coffee. Hours later, when my assistant arrived, we continued with our routine. Later that afternoon, after the children had eaten lunch and napped, I heard the house phone ring. My assistant answered the telephone. She came to where I was and handed me the handset, saying, "It's your husband." Thayer staring at her. I responded with a hello, hearing Israel rambling his words and asking him to slow down and speak clearly.

Once he slowed down, the next thing I heard was "eighteen-month deployment in Baghdad, Iraq," leaving me confused, and I asked, "What happened to the special assignment you mentioned to me about?"

There he couldn't come up with an explanation, leaving me devastated. It wasn't long after finding out what his assignment would be that overwhelmed me, thinking about what was happening in Bagdad. What was the price of the loss of a soldier? It seemed the Defense Department needed more bodies, and they were willing to slaughter more men for a cause I knew nothing about. Yet, at the same time, soldiers were being killed. The thoughts of Israel returning home in a casket with an American flag draped over it bothered me. Needless to say, I remained strong and supported the assignment, even though I didn't want to see it happen.

Although I already knew what was happening in Iraq, watching it on MSNBC Fox News and CNN made me anxious. Unfortunately, our conversation ended shortly after that. There wasn't anything more I wanted to hear. I was crushed, wondering why the Defense did this to us. Knowing Israel had already served twenty-plus years of service to this country didn't make any sense. Haven't the boys and I had enough lost time of not having Israel home? And after hearing Israel would not be coming home, it weighed heavy on my mind.

The more I thought about our memories, the more vivid the visions of him standing in the battleground became. It was not long before I envisioned him standing in the red zone on the battleground.

After sharing the news with my assistant, she said, "It will be all right. You're robust for this kind of stuff."

But was she right? What could happen while Israel was away worried me. However, I had to prepare myself even though my assistant believed everything would be okay.

Once my sons, Mark and Coco, returned home from school and the children went home, I showered, picked up dinner, and returned to feeding the boys before I went to my room.

It was there when I was sitting on the bed, thinking about the boys and Israel. I was saddened, thinking about how much time the boys lost not having their father home. Somehow, the stress began to creep in, overwhelming me at that moment, leaving me in tears, wondering how I would get through Israel's eight months of deployment.

Oddly, when Israel was briefed about his assignment many years after Israel's retirement, I came across Israel's deployment orders that didn't have an ending date but instead said "until" the mission was complete, causing my heart to drop. It would leave me wondering, *What if I was one of the women walking behind his coffin? Will I be broken and numb and in grief? Would I have something to say or be silent, looking out from my veil?* But no matter what I was going through or how I was feeling, one thing was for sure: Throughout my life, I would see my life unable to break apart but would bend low enough to raise myself back up. Whatever was about to happen while Israel was deployed, the only thing I made sure I would do was keep my eyes on our sons, ensuring their youth wouldn't get destroyed by worrying about their father while his boots were standing in the sands of Baghdad, Iraq. When the deployment day arrived, I had to prepare for that big day, leaving my boys home with staff and family.

The Deployment

On the day of my flight, leaving San Antonio, I was up early, packing before making a cup of coffee. Although my trip to Fort Stewart would only be three days, somehow I was bothered leaving the boys home. When my staff arrived, Coco came down and chatted for a while. I gave them a plan and laid some rules. I told Mark to listen to his brother and the adults and that I would be home in a few days before kissing him. He raced back upstairs, seeing him smile like the usual, already dressed for school.

It wouldn't be long before I saw Coco grab my bags, saying, "Mom, we have to go."

I turned, telling my assistant goodbye, and closed the door behind me.

When I arrived at the airport, my makeup had become messy, and I felt like the world had fallen on top of me. But it wouldn't be long before Coco smiled, saying not to worry and to tell Dad how much he loved him. After hearing his words, I knew it was time to exit the car. I grabbed my bags and kissed him goodbye. As I watched Coco drive away, I stood, watching until I couldn't see the roof of his car before entering the airport.

Afterward, I entered the airport at the airline counter to receive my boarding pass and waited at the gate. Waiting, my eyes suddenly became teary, thinking about the boys and Israel. I felt miserable leaving my boys behind, thinking about how I wanted to run. Once my flight was called, I handed the airline employee my boarding pass and entered the cabin, searching for my seat.

When I found where it was, I got to my seat and opened the shed to look out the window. There, looking out the window while the airlines placed things under our plane, my eyes were looking further from where I was sitting, thinking about my boys before the aircraft's wings took me to another ground. I was not prepared to stand on. When I heard the captain's voice, passengers were still boarding the cabin. When all the passengers were on board, I heard the captain's voice again, telling his crew to prepare for departure.

At that moment, I took another look out of the window as I heard the plane gear up. When the captain began to drive the aircraft to where it would be taking off, I watched the other planes line up, feeling the force of the plane flying down the tarmac before the aircraft's wings took us up. The flight to Savannah didn't take long. By noon, my flight touched down, and I followed the passengers down the escalator, where I saw Israel waiting by the pillar.

After kissing me, he asked me to follow him and led me inside a rental agency. After signing the contract, Israel was given the keys, and then we went searching for my bags. When we saw all the luggage was collected and placed at airline security, Israel showed the ticket, and we got my luggage before exiting the airport, searching for the car. At the same time, Israel pressed the keys to locate the vehicle. It didn't take long when he starting the car, asking me to get in.

After Israel kissed me, he placed my bags in the back seat and ask me to follow him.

The time I drove behind Israel didn't take longer than expected, and I was thinking about what would come after once we arrived at the gates of Fort Stewart. While I spent time driving, it wasn't long before I saw Israel's blinkers blinking when we exited.

When we arrived closer to some industrial fences, I felt we were on the grounds of Fort Stewart when I saw an unattended checkpoint. Miles upon miles, I was driving through a forest, passing many deer signs and hoping one didn't run in front of me.

After driving for a while, I became emotional as fear settled within me, and the tears built up before they came flowing out. It wasn't long before I grabbed hold of the knob of the radio and turned it on, hoping to find something to calm me down. Not long after changing the stations, I heard a song I liked as a child by Donna Summer. I began singing, "Toot, hey, beep, beep." Who would've known what the lyrics would be. But no matter what the song was, somehow, that song made me feel better driving the whole way down the forest. It wasn't long from there that I would finally see anything besides woods and trees when I passed through many training camps.

Visioning Israel crawling and getting full of dirt and mud would bring back memories of when Israel was an instructor and would be in the field at Camp Bullis, coming home with muddy BDUs. The thought of hosing down and wringing before placing them in the washer would be something I wouldn't say I liked doing.

The drill of playing war in the forest would prepare Israel and the soldiers he taught. What was to come and what he taught and learned would be used for what awaited him. It wouldn't be long after thinking I would find some relief within myself, filling me with dauntlessness and peace.

Whatever was ahead of me, I wouldn't take for granted whatever was going to happen. I knew I would find my way out of it. But one thing was for sure: It wouldn't be long before I would be seeing myself standing alone on a battlefield.

At the same time, I was passing training camps. We finally arrived at the Fort Stewart's gates. I showed my military ID. The Travelodge wasn't far away. After I parked the car, Israel was right beside the car, opening the door and grabbing my bags. When we arrived upstairs in the room Israel was staying at, he placed my bags on the couch and looked at me, saying, "Let's rent a movie and bring something back to eat."

It would not be long after returning to the car and driving off, when Israel stopped at the shoppette, filled the car with gas, and rented a movie to watch. Shortly after driving to Popeyes, picking up two meals before returning to the Travelodge, we were finally settling in the room, eating and watching the movie that Israel placed in the DVR before we fell asleep in each other arms.

The following morning, I was awakened by Israel's cell phone ringing and saw him sitting on the sofa, placing things inside his duffel bag. Once he saw I was awake, he got up and sat beside me on the bed. Our eyes locked, and he smiled as he continued to speak. There I remained quiet, looking at him, wondering what would happen next. Once Israel hung up the telephone, he asked if I was hungry, and I answered no.

Just as I was getting up, Israel grabbed my arm, turned me around, and told me, "Let's go for a drive so I can show you how to get back to the airport."

It was at that moment my legs dropped, and I hated what I was hearing. That was the last place I wanted to see, and I felt horrible going along with his plans. It wasn't long before Israel kissed me again, and I rushed to the bathroom, falling apart. My thoughts and feeling were scattered, making it harder for me to control them.

After a shower, I saw Israel ready, telling me, he wanted to show me where the continental breakfast was. When we arrived where the breakfast was being served. He helped himself, and I was right there by his side.

After Israel ate, we returned to the room where he would get the keys to the car. It wasn't long before we drove off, feeling woeful, leading me to tears as I stared out the window. Nothing could stop my tears from escaping; my heart was broken, and I was thinking about the boys, knowing how much I missed them, and I couldn't wait to be back home with them. With that being said, when we arrived at Savannah Airport, Israel drove around the manicured grounds before exiting the airport. It would not be long before I heard Israel saying, "Let us go drive around Savanah," leaving me bothered and unable to respond. It felt like Israel was more of a travel guide than a husband. If he was withholding any emotion or feeling, it was hard to detect it.

Even though I had an extremely hard time expressing how I was feeling, the more I refrained from saying anything, the deeper my thoughts sank in. At the same time, the hours were caving in. All the questions I had written would be unanswered, along with overwhelming sadness. However, that day, Israel would not only be driving around Savannah, but we were over a bridge to the beach, where I would get a glimpse of the ocean.

When Israel parked his car, I was in tears, seeing the ocean before me, missing my boys, and feeling vulnerable. Why I was feeling that way, I wouldn't know since I prepared myself for what was to come. When we returned to Fort Stewart, that evening was the same as the day before.

We ate dinner together and watched a movie before falling asleep in his arms.

When the sun rose the following morning, Israel's cell phone rang. I saw Israel dressed in his BDU as I heard his dog tags jittered around his neck. At the same time, he reached for his cell phone. I lay there watching, worried about what would happen. It wasn't long before Israel came and sat beside me, smiling. I felt overwhelmed with the deployment process. No sooner after Israel hung up, he gave me a huge smile, stating it was time to get ready. At that moment, the words that I dreaded to hear were finally weighed down on me, and I hurried toward the shower, where I was pouring out my heart under the showerhead, drowning myself in emotions.

When I felt the water getting cold, I hurried out of the shower, calling out to Israel, and wouldn't hear his voice. Grabbing the towel, I ran out of the bathroom and noticed he was gone. Rushing to get dressed, I hurried to where breakfast was being served and saw him sitting alone in the corner, eating and grabbing a cup of coffee. I went and sat beside him and began noticing the emotion he was feeling. Unsure of what to say, I remained quiet, staring at the clock, feeling vulnerable, trying to think what to do as I looked around the room, seeing many soldiers wearing their uniforms in their desert storm boots, sharing their final hours before leaving for their long-term deployment. Once Israel finished eating, we returned to the room, where he grabbed my arm and turn me around, saying, "This is where I want to leave my goodbyes. Promise me you take care of the boys and yourself while I am away." Then he kissed me again. At that moment, I grabbed him, holding him tighter, telling him not to worry about the boys and me but instead to focus on the mission and coming home safely.

After letting him go, he kissed me again, grabbed his briefcase, reached for an envelope, and handed it to me, saying, "Do not open it until you get word that I am dead." It wasn't until then that tears gushed from my eyes, unsure of what to say as I wiped the tears off, tormented by grief. After handing me his briefcase, he grabbed hold of his duffel bag, taking it to the car. When he returned, his last words were "Let's go," leaving the envelope on the dresser as he carried his briefcase as the door closed behind us.

Once we arrived in the car and drove off, Israel suddenly made a quick U-turn, saying he needed to stop at the company. Smiling, it made me excited, knowing I'd be getting a glimpse of where he worked, and we were given a little more time together. When we arrive at his company, I walked up two flights of stairs and through vinyl curtains, where Israel stopped as he searched for his door key. It wasn't long as I stood standing there when my eyes caught sight of his nameplate, Sgt. Major Martinez. At that moment, I thought about the ups and downs of military life and the ranks he reached in his military career. The thoughts of how much time the boys and I lost with Israel couldn't be replaced. But whatever they were, one thing was for sure: I wasn't prepared for what was going to happen next.

But would there be anything worth losing, knowing life is short at any age? Somehow, I didn't know at that time that I was holding on to the things that mattered the most. It would leave me on my knees.

When Israel finally opened his office door, I followed behind where I would see him reaching under a pile of papers until he found the needed documents.

After handing them for me to hold, he walked toward the corner of the window to pick up the equipment that lay there, smiling, he said, "When I get back from Iraq, I'll clean my office." At that moment, I laughed, thinking he would need a crew to clean up that mess.

Once we returned to the car, we were off to the deployment site, and I was ready for this experience to be over. As we drove up to where the deployment would occur, I saw a woman in uniform with a megaphone, speaking. At that moment, Israel parked under the tree, where he got out, asking me to stay in the car. As I watched and heard the woman speak, I saw Israel standing in a circle with a group of men, unsure of what would happen next. It wasn't long before Israel returned to the car and took his duffel bag and the things he had placed in the car, taking them to where the buses were parked and leaving them there before standing under the tree.

When I heard the woman soldier calling out formation, there were many different emotions when the soldiers began to line up and their names were called. The whole scene was surreal; it wasn't something I was expecting to see. As the soldier lined up by the buses, every man and woman was saluted by the commander and the commanders of the military base. The experience was emotional, and watching Israel standing next to the commander and the officers of Fort Stewart made me feel how sensitive this assignment was. This wasn't just a deployment but a rescue operation to give Iraqi people freedom and aid.

Once every soldier was accounted for and saluted, Israel returned, kissing me the final time, grabbing his briefcase, saying, "Honey, I'll call you when I get a chance." That was the last words I heard before he and his commander boarded the bus. They also saluted before boarding the bus and sat, waving goodbye as the buses' engines geared driving on that rocky road. Finally, the deployment had ended, leaving me in tears as I returned to a lonely room.

Shortly after arriving at the Travelodge, I went straight to bed and wept.

It was hours later when I awakened, calling home to speak to Coco and Mark. Hearing the boys' voices left me excited as my heart filled up with joy. That was all I had left, and there wasn't anything I needed more.

I told them how much I loved them and couldn't wait to see them tomorrow. They handed the phone to my assistant, who asked me how I was feeling. I told her, "I'm making the best with all I have here." I smiled, saying, "I'll feel better when the boys are in my arms."

After I said that, she responded, "Debbie, you have the strength of anybody I don't know. I have seen the strength and love that you show to your children and the children that you teach. You will get through this eighteen-month deployment stronger than you think by raising your family and teaching little ones to grow."

After hearing her say this, I ended our call by saying good night, calling the front desk to set up a wake-up call and going back to sleep. In the morning, I was up right before my telephone rang to wake me up. I showered and dressed.

There, taking a looked around, and the memories I was leaving behind brought back tears as I grabbed the envelope that was left on the counter of the dresser, placing it in my bag, leaving the hotel keys on the dresser, making my way out. After stopping at the storage unit and informing the manager I was about to fly out from Savannah, I checked Israel's units, ensuring they were locked.

After returning to the rental car, I was uptight driving away. It wasn't long before I was lost about which way to go. I made many U-turns and began to cry when suddenly, I ran into a traffic sign pointing toward Savannah. Finally, I was on the interstate, turning on the radio and hearing music to keep going. Unfortunately, while I was driving, I missed my exit and had to keep on driving until I found a place to do a U-turn before I was finally at the airport.

When I arrived at Savannah Airport, I returned to the rental car and hurried to catch my flight. There I had an hour left until it was time to board. When I began thinking about Israel, wondering where he was and if he was all right, I became saddened that it brought me down. I began praying, asking God to watch over my family while Israel was away. I wouldn't know what brought me to that moment. Was it sorrow or worry as my heart broke? What is the chance of Israel getting hurt or killed or something happening to our sons while their father is deployed? That is what I fear the most. Although fear was something I was not used to, somehow, the thoughts of something horrible could have happened. One thing was clear: Something bizarre would happen, and I would be thankful to God.

Once I arrived back in San Antonio later that evening, I heard Mark's voice and saw his head out of the window, calling out to me. Simultaneously, Coco was coming toward me to grab my things. When we arrived home, I gave them both a kiss good night and went to shower before going to bed. In the morning, they were the first ones to awaken, grabbing breakfast as I hurried to get myself dressed right before my students began to arrive for school. There, sipping on my coffee, I felt powerless, like the walls were crashing in. I didn't know why I was feeling this way; however, I promised myself I wouldn't allow fear to invade me no matter what lay ahead.

It took weeks not hearing from Israel. As the days got longer, I stayed updated with all the local news channels about what was happening in Iraq and late breaking news. It would be a few more weeks when the phone rang, when I heard Israel's voice, finally. His words were be quick. He began with, "Honey, I have a few minutes to talk before the phone cuts off for the next person waiting in line." After sharing with me about the conditions he was in, the phone cut off, leaving me in tears.

A couple of days later, Israel got another chance to call home, and this time, he was settling in a trailer with the Internet. Slowly everything was coming together, and soon the Hallmark card came coming. The Internet was the only source I had at my disposal. Getting emails and updates from Israel before leaving to the red zone or going around Iraq with a translator, providing aid to the children and families, was something I never saw happen during the years we have been married. The call of duty came with many assignments, and the nights in the desert would be long. Although when Israel was either in a helicopter or going to the red zone to drop off medical supplies; I always got an email bout his Destination.

Israel was sending photos of him either being inside one of the palaces of Saddam Hussein or helping the people of Iraq and giving food and medical supplies to the families in Iraq, showing the purpose of the mission and the assignment he was ordered to do. Whatever it was to follow, I felt better when I heard him say he was coming home for some R&R (rest and recuperation).

When Israel's flight touched down in San Antonio, he would be in his BDU, placing his backpack in the trunk, getting in the car, and shaking Mark's hand as I drove away. Once we returned home, Coco was there to greet his dad, and they were hugging for the first time he'd been gone.

When the boys went upstairs to their room, Israel went to the bedroom to get ready to shower while I continued to cook. As time passed, Israel came to the dining room with a bag of gifts. There he presented me with a gold bracelet and earrings, while Mark came down to show him his games.

Likewise, Israel will show Mark his bootleg movies, asking him to put one to watch, thereafter calling Coco to come down to eat. Coco returned to his games while Mark, Israel, and I remained watching movies.

It was late in the evening when we went to bed, and for two weeks, he'd been home. The day did come when I had to return him to the airport for his flight back to Iraq. After Israel had a briefing with both of our boys, it didn't take long to wait to hear what was said.

There in the car, Israel leaned toward me, saying, "Promise you wouldn't let Coco join the army." Unsure what he was talking about, his eyes were filled with fear, saying, "Promise me you don't allow him to do this. Young men are getting killed, and I didn't join the United States Army to see my son in the battle zone."

I didn't have time to think about what to say and immediately responded, "Don't worry. I'll make sure he doesn't."

Whatever Coco was planning would send chills up my spine. But one thing was for sure: He wouldn't know while I was driving his daddy to the airport, I'd be planning something to take Coco's mind from getting enlisted.

While Israel's mind was worrying about Coco, we had finally arrived at the airport. After leaning over to kiss me, he grabbed hold of his backpack, exited the car, shut the car door, and went around reminding me about Coco. I told him not to worry, kissed him, drove off, looked back in the rearview mirror, taking my last look from behind. During my drive home, I was thinking about what to do with Coco and how to keep him busy. In finding solutions, I called my sister, asking if Coco could spend the weekends at her home to play video games with the boys. It sounded like my problem was solved; however, it wouldn't be long before the problem became my nightmare.

Although I couldn't devise ways to keep him safe and busy, I sat him down, talked to him in his room, informing him of what his dad shared with me. Giving him a little more freedom to drive around in his car when he wasn't working, I told Coco he could drive to see his cousin in Elmendorf with one condition: he wouldn't drive late or early in the wee morning hours.

The fear of giving Coco more freedom worried me; however, I knew I promised Israel I wouldn't allow Coco to make a choice to join the military after hearing what was happening to the young men that were serving in Iraq.

Coco was driving every weekend to and from Elmendorf. A day came when I heard a man's voice saying he was with the San Antonio police and couldn't find the insurance for the car. I asked him if it was in the compartment in the car, and he said it wasn't there. I asked him where the car was and was told at Flying J on Forster Road. After telling the police officer I was on my way, I hurried off of the bed, put on my robe and slippers, checked on Mark before I bolted to Flying J.

After locking the door, I drove up the hill and caught sight of flashing lights and saw flares directing vehicles moving in the center of the lane. When I arrived closer to the police cars, I saw half of Coco's car beneath the semitruck and an ambulance yards away. Hurrying to park the car, I ran toward the ambulance. When I got inside the ambulance, I saw Coco lying on a gurney, surrounded by paramedics.

There I yelled out, "Coco, Coco," when suddenly he responded, asking, "What had happened?" At that moment, I gave him a crazy look.

"Why don't you tell us what happened?"

During that time, he couldn't remember. I then got out of the ambulance and went to speak to the officers at the scene, handing him the insurance card. I took a better look at the wreck. I was disturbed by what I see, relieved that my son was still alive and nobody else was with him in the car. Once everything settled down, I returned to the ambulance to check on Coco and was told he had a two-inch gash on his head.

When the police officers completed their investigation, a tow truck arrived to pick up the scattered parts on the road once the semitruck was handed with the information about the car insurance. The officers returned and handed the insurance card back, along with the care of my son. It was at that moment that anxiety hit me, and I was saying, "Oh, no, I don't think so." I got nervous when I see blood and preferred that my son be taken to BAMC by the paramedics so they could care for him after running into a monster truck. Thayer, handling the officers Coco's military ID. I returned home, got dressed, and checked on Mark before going to the hospital.

Once I arrived at the hospital, Coco was placed in a neck brace, complaining about his headache, and the two-inch gash wound was cleaned. When the physician returned, I was told that the X-rays and CT scans looked great, and they began to stitch the wound while Coco complained about his headache. It was then when I reacted, telling him, "That's what happens when you run into a semitruck," smiling, thanking the doctors. We arrived home later in the morning. I gave another pill for Coco's headache before going to bed.

When I awakened in the morning, Mark would be up playing games, and Coco fast asleep. That afternoon, I called the insurance company to file a claim. It was later when the telephone rang, and I was talking to Israel about the car wreck. After describing the car's details, it dawned on me, remembering how the car was, noticing the driver seat was in the center and the hatchback hovering over the seat, which never shattered, not far from being killed. For Coco to walk away with a two-inch stitched left me baffled. However, I was grateful that nobody else was with him in the car at midnight. After hanging up the telephone with Israel, Coco realized that he was carless, and I would be the person driving him to work until another car was purchased.

It would be days later when I went to Alamo Body Shop to meet the insurance adjuster. When we were taken to where the car was sitting, the agent removed the tarp. He gasped, saying, "No one died in this accident?"

Coco began to laugh, cracking up; I think it's a teen-age thing."

The adjuster said, "Someone loves you up there."

It dawned on me the prayer I prayed in Savannah Airport, asking God to watch over the boys while Israel was deployed would save me. I wouldn't know what condition I would be if I had lost my son, but I knew this time that I had to keep a closer eye on him and set limits when it came to driving in the early morning hours. After the adjuster completed the claim and issued us a check, we returned home.

Days later, we went searching to purchase another vehicle. This time I made sure it came with a curfew and cruise control. Days later, I would receive a copy of the police report and the settlement that the insurance paid to the semitruck owner, which was estimated nearly over fifty thousand dollars. As far as the police report. The report detailed that Driver A (Coco) fell asleep at the wheel, hitting Driver B (semitruck car driver), causing the car to spin around before sliding underneath Driver B.

Weeks later, Israel told me he was retaining to attend Coco's graduation, and I would be preparing to open my first day care facility. Once Israel returned to Iraq, the boys and

I would be getting the facility ready for inspection. And on Halloween, I would receive my childcare license. It wouldn't be long being at the center that Coco would surprise me with a marriage license. Yes, I was officially a mother-in-law, which I never saw that one coming.

When Israel learned Coco was married, he said we should've allowed him to join the military. At that point, he was already a man with a wife, and there wasn't anything we can do. Coco's wife was sweet, quiet, shy, and beautiful. He didn't need anything, leaving me in peace that he was safer being married, keeping him from driving back and forth to Elmendorf.

During the holidays, Israel spent Thanksgiving, Christmas, and New Year, celebrating them in Baghdad, Iraq. The thought of Israel ever returning back from deployment only intensified when spring of the flowers would bloom and my business remained successful.

In the month of March, the telephone rang, and it was the commander's wife, stating our husbands were coming home. The thoughts of why I did not hear the good news from Israel made me wonder. However, I was grateful to hear that my baby was returning home. No sooner after hanging up the telephone, the phone rang again, and it was from the Fort Stewart Headquarters, informing of the return of my husband. After hearing three "Infantry Davison is returning home," I hanged up and rushed to the computer to check my emails and didn't see one waiting from Israel.

It would be a half hour later when the telephone rang again when I heard the voice of Israel, saying, "Honey, I'm coming home."

When the time came for the Third Infantry Division to return home, Israel planned for me to welcome him. Once my plane tickets and car rental were reserved, I was counting the days until I finally let go of the fear of him being in the red zone. Although Israel was returning to Fort Stewart, I was excited when I saw him retire after the deployment.

At the time Israel and his unit were preparing to return home, Israel called to ask me to search for a hotel for us to stay in, unaware of how strenuous it would be.

Third Infantry Division Returns Home

At the time Israel's unit was preparing to return home to Fort Stewart, he already had everything prepared for my arrival on the day of my flight out from San Antonio.

I was packing when I saw my sister-in-law dressed, going to the kitchen. When I finished packing, I went to the kitchen and spoke to her. At the time, we were talking about the day care. It wouldn't be long when Coco and his wife came downstairs. I shared with them the plans I wanted them to follow. At the time we were discussing the plans, I heard, "Mom, Mom" and saw Mark running downstairs. At that moment, he was asking for money. I asked how much he needed, and immediately he said one hundred dollars for games.

There, I asked him how many he could purchase for one hundred dollars. He quickly answered how many he could buy with the money after handing Mark the hundred-dollar bill. When Mark ran back upstairs to get ready for school, I looked at my sister-in-law and asked her to take Mark to GameStop.

When my sister-in-law left to open the facility, I saw Coco picking up my bags, saying it was time to go. I took my last look around. I saw Mark and my daughter-in-law standing at the top edge of the stairs. I said goodbye, giving Mark my last words, "Listen to your brother," as he kissed me goodbye before closing the door. When I arrived at the car, I began to feel sad as tears clouded my eyes before exiting. Even though feeling an emotional, my heart was divided: whether I wanted to get out of the car and run to Mark or return to Georgia and wait to arrive on the grounds of Fort Stewart for Israel. However, I had my hand on the car door handle. The thought of not being there to welcome him home crushed me.

When Coco arrived at the San Antonio Airport, I was emotionally drained. It didn't take long before Coco said, "Don't worry, Mom, I'll keep an eye on Mark." That's when I felt this was going to be okay. I had Coco and knew I could trust him to watch over Mark. After speaking for a little while, I wiped my tears off and kissed him goodbye before grabbing my bags from the back seat as he drove off, standing until I no longer saw the roof of his car.

Upon entering the airport, I went to the airline to check in, received my boarding pass, and sat at the terminal until the time came for me to board.

When my flight arrived in Savannah, I went to pick up my luggage before getting the rental car, feeling afflicted by not being home with my boys. Once I picked up the rental car, I turned on the radio to find a channel to distract me from my regret. It wasn't long after changing the channels that I ran into Christian music. I listened to it, feeling like I could get through all things. Who would know, on that day and that time, all things in my life would be turned upside down. Get ready. This is going to be a long ride. When I arrived at the hotel and checked in, the stayovers weren't so much, not nonexistent. As I listened to the front desk associate explain that the Third Infantry Division was returning and didn't have any hotels available for the extra nights, I thought, *How will Israel make a way out of this mess?*

When the front desk clerk gave me the room key, I got on the elevator and went to my room. There I changed into comfortable clothes and went searching for Fort Stewart. Upon arriving at the entrance of the gates of Fort Stewart, I asked where they were hosting the welcoming ceremony and was told to follow the signs, and just like that, I would be sitting in the fields of Cottrell, visioning that exciting moment.

I drove away from Cottrell and picked a few things and a bottled water at the commissary. After paying, I returned to the hotel and called home to check everything happening there. When I heard everything was going as planned, I got into my pajamas, turned on the television, and fell asleep.

The following morning, after awakening, I called home and spoke to Coco and my sister-in-law to check on Mark. After hearing Mark was doing well, I hung up and watched the news when I heard about the welcoming ceremonies that would happen at the gates of Fort Stewart. When I saw it was time for me to rise to get dressed, I would run to the ice machine, filling my bucket of ice before stepping into the tub. After taking a hot bath, I got dressed, removed the "Do not disturb" from the door, and made my way down to the lobby.

When the elevator doors opened, I saw the foyer filled with people with signs and American flags. At that moment, the welcoming ceremony represented more than just their return but also the loss of time being so far away with little contact, unsure of their daily whereabouts.

You couldn't imagine how hard it was to get through eighteen months, supporting a mission with a deadly price.

It wasn't long after taking my eyes off the signs and the excited families that I rushed to the car to be first out of the parking lot. When I arrived at the gates of Fort Stewart, I was excited. Once I reached the fields of Cottrell, I sat on the bleachers. There, watching the children running and playing on the grounds brought back memories.

Although our sons were older, they wouldn't be here to see the grounds of Stewart filled with excitement while we waited for the buses to arrive. As the time clock kept ticking, the commander spoke, informing us that our loved ones had arrived and that they were boarding. Everyone began to cheer. After he had given the families updates, he asked us to cheer the loudest; pointing to the vast television placed on Cottrell's grounds. There we were, practicing until he got off the megaphone, and the music began playing on Cottrell's fields.

While I sat and waited for the buses to arrive, I overheard two military wives speaking about their husbands' deployment and the challenges they endured during their spouses' absence. Considering the possibilities a servicemember could face, the difficulties of having one parent home with young children being exhausting and overwhelming. Being a daughter and wife of a servicemember, the only thing I could say is, if I didn't work or be busy, I don't know how I would survive this deployment alone.

While I staring at the children that were playing, it didn't take long before I heard the commander's voice again, saying, "Our soldiers are here." I was looking at the television monitor as the soldiers were lining up behind the large trees on Cottrell, and the noise on the grounds became louder.

Looking at this vast TV monitor, it captured the ceremony. It wouldn't be long before I heard the commander welcome the soldiers back on the grounds of Fort Stewart. I saw the soldiers moving shoulder to shoulder, making their way out of the trees. The sounds of cheering and screams settled within me, a feeling I could not explain. Although I was saddened knowing some families didn't get to see this day, my heart was filled with feelings seeing those babies running to their parent/parents, for they waited so long for this day. Then suddenly, the song "God bless the USA," by Lee Greenwood was played as the company flags waved on the grounds of Stewart, bringing me to tears. I didn't know what to do next as I felt my body crushed, thinking about the families that lost the most.

Whatever happened after the deployment would be unseen, but knowing Israel was home on US soil, I knew we would return where we left off.

After the song was finished, I heard Israel's voice calling me, and I came down the bleachers, smiling before our lips touched, kissing him. Showing him where I parked the car, I handed him the car keys as he drove back to where the buses were parked to collect his duffel bag and things, then went to the hotel where we would remain for a few days.

A few days later, Israel and I went to the storage unit to check on the household goods he had placed in storage before stopping at the apartment rental agency. That day would be one that caught us off guard. After entering the apartment agency, we were told that there wasn't any apartment or homes available for rent. At that moment, we looked at each other and became concerned about what to do next.

After leaving the rental agency, Israel decided to drive to Savannah, searching for an apartment closer to the military base. It wouldn't be long while we were going to Savannah when my eyes caught sight of an apartment complex when we were exiting off the interstate.

Excited, I didn't take my eyes off the apartment complex, thinking they would have apartments available. I noticed their well-maintained units and the manicured landscape surrounding the property once Israel parked the car. When we entered the apartment management office, a woman greeted us. At the same time Israel was inquiring about an apartment, we were taken to her office and was told what he had available to lease. She shared that she didn't have one bedroom available until five weeks from today. Suddenly, Israel would lean over, asking me if I could stay a little longer to assist him with the move. At that moment, I couldn't answer; the thoughts of being away from my boys and business weighed heavy on my heart.

Though I had to give him an answer, *my heart was already at no, but I knew that Israel counted on me to help him.* I asked Israel to wait a few minutes. I called my sister-in-law, asking her if she could continue watching the boys and my business until Israel was settled into his apartment. Just like that, she agreed, and I would be spending many more weeks between Hinesville and Fort Stewart, Georgia. Later that afternoon, after Israel signed the apartment contacted, we returned to the hotel, packing and relocating from motel to motel until finally we could get a room reserved at the travel lodge on Fort Stewart.

Once we settled back to the travel lodge, Israel returned to the storage unit, picking up the car he placed in storage. After he cranked up the car, the storage unit was filled with smoke, and I was coughing and laughing, trying not to wet my pants. At the same time, he is pressing on the gas. The storage manager and her assistant came running in with a fire extinguisher, thinking there was a fire. When she noticed Israel pressing the gas pedal, she began coughing, asking Israel to stop and turn the car off.

Shortly after Israel did that, the smoke and fumes faded away. It wasn't long before the unit manager told Israel to drive the smoky car on the interstate until the gas and fumes were out.

Who would've thought that wasn't going to work? While I was driving behind Israel, the smoke would have people around him stop as he returned to the grounds with Smoky. Israel went around Fort Stewart. While the smoke followed behind him, the fire department arrived at the travel lodge after someone called in that a car was burning, before buying another car, selling the smoky Joe to another soldier.

The weeks that followed while Israel wasn't working, we spent weekends at a movie theater or visiting a restaurant while waiting for the apartment. By then, I was ready to go home, and my arms wrapped around my boys.

On the day of the move, Israel was up early. After saying "let's eat breakfast before picking up the U-Hall," we went. And after returning to the hotel room, Israel went alone to pick up the U-Hall, while I remained in the room. When he returned, we left the room and went to the storage unit. Shortly after arriving, we began removing boxes when Israel's cell phone rang, and I heard a woman calling from Mark Middle School.

It was Mark's teacher, and she stated she was concerned about Mark. She said Mark fell and hit the desk. I was unsure what she meant he fell and what she was talking about. I kept listening to her before cutting her off, asking where Mark was, and was told he was sent home with one of my family members. After learning he was home and safe, I replied that I'd be home this weekend and would have Mark see his physician on Monday. Long after hanging up with her, I called home to check up on Mark, and my daughter-in-law said he was asleep. I also contacted my sister-in-law to ask who picked Mark up from school and took him home. While speaking to my sister-in-law, I asked her if Mark had been acting differently lately, and she said no.

Unsure of what the teacher was talking about, I told my sister-in-law to keep an eye on him, and I would see her on Sunday. After hanging up, I stood with the broom in my hand, wondering what was happening with Mark, fearing something was wrong. I was feeling more worried about it than before. Whatever was happening, it was out of my control.

The time thinking about Mark needing me had bothered me, and I was wondering what to do. When Israel walked out from the storage unit, our eyes met, and he asked, "What's wrong?"

I said, "I don't know, but something wasn't right." I shared with Israel what Mark's teacher said. He asked where Mark was, and I immediately said he was home, asleep. I thought that would make me feel better, but somehow, it didn't, and I regretted being so far away from him.

When all the boxes and furniture were placed in the U-Hall, we drove to the apartment complex and parked, then removed some boxes and took them to the third floor. We sat inside the U-Hall while Israel devised a plan on how to get the couch into his third floor of his apartment. After listening to his ridiculous plan, I went to the couch, turned it on its side, lifted it, placed it on my backside, and made my way up the stairs, while Israel held it at the end. When we finally made it inside the apartment, I squatted, leaving it on its side before giving Israel my last two words, "I'm tired," and went to lie down on the floor, leaving Israel to finish up. After placing the household goods into the apartment, we return the U-Hall to the company.

The following day, I awakened seeing Israel unpacking boxes. There I was asked if I wanted breakfast and answered no, telling him I wanted to go home. After he heard me express I wanted to go home, his replied, "You be home tomorrow." It seemed Israel didn't have the same feeling as I had not being home with our boys. However, his actions affected me in many ways, changing my feeling about the situation. As the hours ticked by, I felt horrible not being home and away from Mark.

On my last day in Savannah, my day began rough, While Israel did his best to convince me to eat something, nothing he could've done and said would satisfy me as I remained wrapped in the blankets until noontime. The thought of staying in bed worried Israel. Although I wasn't interested in anything he was doing to make me feel better, it made me feeling terrible not trying to make our last day together memorable. When I was ready to arise from bed, I dressed and accompanied him to a restaurant to eat a late lunch, unaware of what Israel would do next. After eating, we crossed the bridge to the beach. Tears were streaming from my face, thinking about Mark.

I heard Israel say, "Let's go for a walk on the beach."

Tears ran down my face, asking him to take me back to the apartment. It wouldn't be long before I arrived at the apartment. I returned to bed and waited for that night to be over.

I got up and dressed the following morning, ready to return home. Once Israel took my luggage to the car, I grabbed my headphone and listened to music, while Israel drove me to the airport. When I arrived at Savannah Airport and checked in, I kissed Israel goodbye and hurried to the terminal, waiting for my flight to be called. When I was finally seated in the plane cabin, I put on my seat belt and looked out of the window, excited to be returning home.

Coco was waiting for me at the airport when I arrived that afternoon. After placing my luggage in the trunk, I asked Coco to hand over the car keys, I summoned Coco, saying, "Don't do what you see me do." I grabbed the keys and got into the driver's seat and sped away until I reached the corner of my street and hurried upstairs to check on Mark.

When I saw Mark on his bed, playing video games, I saw numerous scratches and abrasions on his face. I asked Coco to go downstairs and bring me the peroxide, ointment, and cotton balls. After cleaning all the wounds on Mark's face, I asked him if he remembered how he got these scratches and cuts. Smiling, he answered, "I fell, Mom." After hearing he had some recollection, I told him he didn't have to get up early for school. I was planning to have him examined by a doctor at the adolescent clinic. I kissed him. As I returned downstairs, I was wondering how a fourteen-year-old could sustain so many marks on his face and in the back of his head without anyone providing me some explanation.

But whatever they didn't tell me, I was about to witness the aftermath of a mother's broken heart. The following morning, I got up and went to open the day care for the first time after returning back from my trip. When the central appointment was open, I called and made a doctor's appointment for Mark. When I was given a time from central appointment, I called home, asking my daughter-in-law to ensure Mark was up and dressed when I arrived.

Later that afternoon, I went home and picked up Mark for his doctor's appointment. When we arrived at the clinic and he was checked, we watched the television while I began to think about my conversation with his teacher, unsure of what she meant by "bells are setting him off." I turned my attention to Mark, staring at him, wondering what the teacher saw. I didn't see it. Mark looked healthy while watching television while he sat there next to me. But that was about to change in an instant.

When Mark's name was called, we were placed in one of the examination rooms where he would be sitting on the examining table. I sat on the chair, waiting for the doctor to arrive, when I heard a knock on the door. The doctor came in and sat next to me, asking what brought us in today. Not knowing how to start the conversation, I began with, "I was out of town when Mark's teachers called me to say, bells were setting him off, causing him to fall." Shortly after giving her that information, she began to ask Mark if he drank alcohol or smoked. He told her no. After asking Mark all sorts of questions, she began her examination. She turned off the light and placed the ophthalmoscope in Mark's eyes, then I screamed, asking, "What was that?" She called me over and asked me not to move from his side. Mark was having a monoclinic seizure. Tears flooded my eyes. I was upset, wondering what was happening to him, while the doctor told me to stay where I was while she went and got help.

It felt like hours after a few minutes of standing there with Mark. I was worried; I didn't know what I should do if he went into another seizure. It would not take long as I kept my eyes on him, leaving me grief-stricken about what had happened to him while I was away.

When I saw the room door opened, I saw the doctor with a neurologist. I was asked about Mark's medical history. I told him about Mark, between 5 and 6 years old, when diagnosed with epilepsy and treated and was reevaluated and taken off the medicine by his PCM when he was in third grade and was seizure-free for many years. Mark had a normal life. He enjoyed playing games, riding his scooter and bike, and loved shadowing his brother and his friends. He was always happy playing games and going to school. The thoughts of watching him would affect me emotionally.

Mark was admitted into the hospital, while the doctors tried different medicines to help his condition. It would be weeks that I was by his side, ensuring he was cared for while my heart cracked, seeing him this way, leaving me wondering why this happened. After weeks of taking Mark to all of his appointments, we went to Houston at the Baylor Children Hospital. After spending a few days there, we returned home with no answers.

The stress overwhelmed me that I decided to shut my childcare center and relocate my license back to my residence, reopening a licensed group home, while the staff kept my business going. Weeks turned into months. Mark became highly medicated while the doctors tried other medications to get him back to his feet. Being unable to do more for him, it would numb me, forcing me to take it one day at a time. All I could do at that moment was keep my eyes on him, feeling powerless as a mom, crying, thinking about the possibility of waking up and seeing he was gone while it felt like a long nightmare that lasted forever.

During that time, I was taking Mark to his doctor's appointments. There was one appointment that left me heartbroken. It was the day when Dr. A scheduled a procedure for Mark with his team. Watching the procedure, I stood away from the operating table while Dr. A looked from behind. As one of the teams of doctors began a spinal fluid procedure, I heard Mark's crying, and I became emotional seeing how the doctor kept going in and out with the needle, causing me to react. It was there that I asked the doctor to stop, saying, "Don't you see him crying?"

After responding and asking the doctor to stop, he approached me, saying, "You people don't get it."

I immediately responded, unsure what he meant, "What is it my people don't get?"

Suddenly, he said to me, "There's nothing more we can do for your son," leaving me helpless. After staring at the team of doctors standing around, I looked at Dr. A, wiping off my tears. Then one of the women doctors asked if I wanted an advocate. Looking at her, I said, "No, we're leaving," getting Mark back into his wheelchair, taking him to the car where I wept.

When we returned home, I placed Mark back and began thinking about what to do. Weeks went by, then the next school year began, and I would arrive at the middle school searching for answers to what happened to my son and wanting to see the report by the nurse who treated him. Upon entering, the administration was on their toes when they saw me coming in the door, asking to speak to the nurse.

Then I was told that the nurse was on her way. I saw the principal's door opening, and she was leaning. I wondered why she was so interested in hearing my conversation.

When the nurse arrived in the office, I asked for a copy of Mark's incident report, and she told she didn't have it and that his records were sent to the district office. Unaware of why they weren't at the school concerned me. While she continued to speak, I stopped her, asking how long it would take to get a copy and was told next week. I let her know I would come back for it, leaving her there while the principal and her staff watched as I left. After returning home, I was searching for another doctor for Mark while waiting for the nurse's report. When the weekend ended, I went back to Mark's middle school and saw the principal turning around, running the other way. I caught up with her, standing at the nurse's office.

Thinking what to say, I asked the nurse for Mark's incident report. She went around me to where her computer was and printed me a copy. I was thinking why she gave me that excuse that Mark's file was at the district office. I briefly examining the report she just handed me. What I saw terrified me. He had fallen many times, which began around winter. Majority said they had applied ice and sent him back to the classroom.

In reviewing the document, I saw Mark's final days in school, explaining his condition before leaving the school. I told them, "How dare you keep this from me and calling local authorities on me," and left to show the document to Dr. A. After he looked at the document, he asked, "The school gave you this?" After saying yes, he called the school, seeking answers. The negligence of the school not informing me about Mark's health blew my mind away. And due to the lack of their responsibilities, the falls that Mark sustained over the months worsened over time, leading to his medical problems. Afterward, I returned home just in time to give Mark his medicine and file a complaint to the TEA (Texas Education Association), and fought for Mark's rights to bring him back to his feet, trying not to allow the stress to destroy me.

It would be fall when I decided to write the president of the United States, Mr. Obama, sharing the story about my son Mark and my husband's deployment in Baghdad, Iraq. I wanted him to know the feeling I had being a wife of a deployed soldier. I expected no honor but respect being a married wife, managing a family household while my husband was serving this country. Days later, I would receive a letter from President Obama with links and numbers for me to seek help. After speaking to the Department of Education in Washington, it wasn't long when everything began to move on Mark's behalf. I finally saw justice for Mark. When I received a call from Region 20 saying that they contacted the middle school and was given a week to find a homebound teacher for Mark, unaware it would take them a few days to accomplish that. When I received a call for Mark's school, they were excited with the news that they found a teacher for

Mark, and his name was Mr. Justice. It would be later when I would hear how they were able to moved so fast.

While I was taking Mark from one appointment to another, Israel said that their unit was called for a second deployment to Baghdad, and he had two weeks to get ready. During that time, Israel would have a flight ready for Coco to assist him in storing all of his things into storage.

When the time came that order was called, I returned to Savannah with the little bit of energy I had, leaving Coco and my daughter-in-law caring for Mark. What felt like a quick in-and-out visit would be painful seeing my life play out from something of a Lifetime movie, although my visit in Stewart would be short. It brought back painful thoughts. I didn't return home sooner. The thoughts of something worse to happen didn't settle well within me, making me a little paranoid. I pushed myself to rise from the rocking chair to meet Coco at the car.

When I arrived at Savannah, I went back at the Travelodge in Fort Stewart, just like the last time I came with dinner in the room and watched a movie, although this time, Israel had many bootleg movies for me to choose from that he brought from his first deployment. It wasn't the movies that was tiring me out; it was the strain of nerves that was on my mind, thinking of Mark.

When the sun rose the following morning, Israel's cell phone rang, and I knew the hour came and had arrived to get dressed. I hurried to the shower. It wouldn't be long before I came out of the shower and saw Israel gone. When I got dressed, I went to where the continental breakfast was being served, and we shared our last hour together.

Within the few minutes, we enjoyed our meal together, knowing it would be short. It wasn't long after sitting at the table that I would see the sadness on Israel's face. Somehow,

I tried not to face whatever was bringing him down. I knew we both were thinking about Mark, and it was hurting him, not knowing if he would ever get better. If he was going to get past his fears of what he was leaving behind, he had to remember, I had this, and we were waiting for his return.

When we returned to the hotel room, Israel picked up his duffel bag and grabbed his briefcase as the room closed behind him. When we arrived at the deployment site, the mood was quiet, and a few children were present as Israel checked in. It wasn't long before Israel returned to the car, showing me his assigned weapons, an AK-47 and a handgun attached to a holding belt, leaving me uncomfortable. Sitting in the car together, he grabbed my hand and squeezed it. Once I looked into his eyes, tears began to flow out of them. When he squeezed them again, I began to feel he didn't want to let me go leaving defeated. At that time, I didn't know what to say or do to improve the situation. It wouldn't be long before Israel and the soldiers in his company boarded the bus to accept things as they were and find a finer way to get through them.

As time passed, remembering Israel's last words "I love you" felt like an arrow piercing me. When I returned home to San Antonio, I continued my duties, caring for Mark.

A few weeks later, I heard the telephone ring. As the phone rang, it left me paralyzed and frighten, wondering who was calling while it continued to ring. I arose, answering the telephone, asking what happened. When I heard my little brother's voice, his first words were, "Why is it every time I call you, you always say 'what happened?'" I was unsure why he was bothered. Then he told me, "Mom's dead and died in a car accident."

I asked him where Mom was. He told me he was in the hospital, that his wife was in surgery then hung up. I called him back and didn't get an answer.

At that moment, after hearing the horrible news at midnight, I was hoping it was a dream, but I was feeling numb. I went back to the couch and cried out to Mom, reminder her that Mark was still sick. The feeling that my brother was sitting in the hospital, not knowing the whereabouts of our mother, it would leave me feeling upset that I could not do more.

When the hour came and I knew I needed to rise up, I called the sheriff's department in Maricopa in Phoenix, getting information. After making contact with the police department, I was told that the detectives were out, and I could leave a message. I called my brother several times. He was not answering my calls. I reached out to American Red Cross for help relocating the whereabouts of Israel in Baghdad, leaving my name and number shortly after hanging up.

I returned to the couch, sitting in the dark, thinking which sibling I would contact first. I couldn't believe this was happening as the tears poured out from my eyes, calling out for Mom. When three o'clock came, I was drained with all kinds of emotions.

At six o'clock, I called my little sister, telling her "Mom is dead." When she heard me, she asked what happened, and I was too hurt to answer, leaving me no option but to hang up.

The pain of feeling Mom was gone overwhelmed me. And when I contacted my older brother and sister, I left the message with their employers.

A few hours later, when my assistant arrived, she saw me deeply upset, asking what happened to Mark, unaware it wasn't about him. I began to cry, saying that my mother was gone; she passed away in a car accident. In that moment, I was back in grief, thinking that I was just talking to her a few days ago, and now she was gone and wasn't coming back. I couldn't get passed the grief and the heartbreak as I looked at Mark sleeping in the room, crying, wondering how I would get through the pain. The crying tormented me, missing my mother and knowing Mark's illness was critical and the whereabouts of Israel unknown.

When my assistant took the student to the classroom, the phone rang again, and it was my oldest sister. I confirmed with her that, yes, Mom was gone before telling her I didn't know what to do. She told with me about a funeral home near the house our mother once owned, where I would meet her later that afternoon. When I arrived, my sister was waiting as we walked into the funeral home together.

At the same time, we waited for the grief counselor. We were brought into a room when the grieves counselor came walking in. There he provided the cost of a full funeral and all other expenses. Suddenly, my sister said, "We could have Mom cremated."

Listening to her suggestion, I thought about Mom, what she would've wanted, and the life she gave to all of us before asking the grief counselor to add up the total, writing a check, and leaving my sister there to select Mom's flowers for her funeral after returning home. I made arrangements to fly to Phoenix and bring Mom back home. When Israel heard the news about my mother, he called home and said he couldn't leave to be with me after arriving at the red zone.

The following morning, I arrived in Phoenix three days before Valentine's Day. I exited the plane cabin, thinking the first person I would see would be my little brother. Well, I was wrong. Instead, I'd be in tears, trying to reach him on his cell phone, and he wouldn't answer.

It was at that moment that left me upset, wondering why he wasn't answering his phone. The thoughts of why he was doing this now when he knew I would be arriving made my relationship with him stressful, leaving a horrible feeling. I was alone in an unfamiliar place, feeling this was the last thing he needed to worry about. It would be many minutes later when my cell phone rang, and I heard my brother's voice, asking me to write down the address for me to go to.

When I arrived at the address he had given, I was unaware that I was entering a law firm. Once I entered the building, a receptionist asked if I was Debra Martinez, taking me to the second floor and telling me to sit in a huge conference room. There she offered me water, telling me my brother and his lawyer would be here shortly.

Unaware of what my brother was up to, the thought of him having me drive to a law firm made my blood boil. You couldn't imagine how upset I was feeling. There I was, thinking about Mom as tears flowed, looking at my brother, his wife, and the lawyer.

"Our mother isn't buried yet, and you bring me to a law firm?"

When I arose out of my chair, I told them, "I don't know what game my brother is playing, but no one is going to profit from her mother's death until her funeral expenses are paid in full." It felt like I was lit on fire. I stormed out, pressing the elevator button and hearing my brother's excuses before cutting him off, saying, "How dare you do this to me. I waited for you at the airport, and you bring me here." I left him standing, returned to the car, and waited for them to come out.

When my brother and his wife exited the law firm, I drove to their house where Mom was living. And though the gravel and dirt road, I came to their residence and saw the mountains behind the house. After entering the home, I was escorted to her room and saw many outfits she purchased before her death as tears flooded my eyes. I looked out of the window, thinking about the mountain she mentioned to me right before her death. I heard my brother telling me to take anything I wanted in the room.

I replied, "I only came for an outfit for Mom's funeral, her pictures, and the picture of the pope that belonged to our sister."

They both walked out from Mom's room, leaving me alone.

As I stood, staring out of Mom's window, I remembered the tone of her voice, how excited she was describing the mountains she would see throughout her day, leaving me in tears remembering her last words.

As I continued to think about it, it brought me to tears knowing I would never see her or hear her voice again. My brother and his wife returned, handing me a purse, saying, "Mom told me to give this to you when you come to get her."

I asked, "Mom knew I was coming?" Although she knew something was about to arise, one thing was for sure: it would leave her in shock.

They were unable to answer my question. I grabbed the purse and an outfit, taking it to the car. When I returned to her room, I gathered her pictures and the poster, taking them to the car. Then I hugged my little brother, telling him, "Let's meet for coffee before going to see Mom at the funeral home."

That would be the last I returned to my brother's house, driving away from the rocky road as tears rolled out from my eyes, feeling Mom walking over the mountain, excited, remembering her last words. That would be the only memory that brought some peace. Although her eyes made her path, what would hurt the most would be not having the chance to say goodbye.

Before arriving at the hotel to check in, I was speaking to one of my closet friends that called to see how I was doing. I would be reframing, telling her, "Like running my car into a wall." I would be wondering if she knew I was joking about that attempt, which I thought would be severe just hours earlier. Although the pain was attacking me in several ways, what people didn't know is that the sorrow I was going through began many months earlier with Mark.

When I arrived to the hotel room, I showered. It wasn't long when I began crying, thinking about tomorrow. I got up to get something to eat. And when I returned to the room, I vomited. After changing my clothes, I lay half off the bed with my long hair dripping downward toward the floor, feeling horrible. The thought of Mark being ill and Mom gone and Israel on the battlefield in Iraq left me powerless, feeling no way out, making it incredibly difficult, paralyzing me.

The following morning, I arose to get dressed to meet my brother for coffee. But before arriving to see him, I drove to the Maricopa Police Department to talk to the detective. After arriving at the police department, I was told she was out, leaving me upset and wouldn't return anytime soon. I went back to the car. Just taking a few minutes of crying, I felt broken, missing the last opportunity to speak to the detective who was handling my mother's death. Regardless of the situation, all of my questions would be left unanswered, leaving me upset.

When I arrived at the restaurant, my brother and his wife was waiting. After ordering myself a cup of coffee, I heard my brother's wife sharing the accounts of her tragically accident. She began her story with Mom wanting Mexican food and how she and Mom drove to pick it up. When they were returning home, a car stopped in front of them, causing her to swirl before rolling down a ditch. My first thoughts were, why she didn't just hit the car, making me upset. If she had hit the car, Mom might've been alive today. However, who knows. But after I saw the reaction on my brother's and sister-in-law's faces, my stomach turned with sadness, thinking that they seemed they were more like bystanders than victims of my mother's death.

Although it would leave me upset, the actions of my sister-in-law, in my eyes, made me sick to my stomach; telling them it was time to go. When we arrived at the funeral home, the grief counselor was waiting. When he briefed us about the injuries Mom sustained, I prepared myself for the worse before entering the viewing room. When the grief counselor opened the door, I saw Mom on a gurney in her hospital clothes. There watching my brother and his wife as they went to see her. I was crying for serval minutes, holding on to her outfit. When I got the strength to move forward, I went forward with a shield of power, with my eyes focused on my brother as he and his wife were combing Mom's hair with their hands. As they stood smiling, talking about her and the memories they had, I was crying, seeing with my own eyes that she was *gone and isn't coming back,* crushing me inside. After noticing the abrasions she suffered, I was on fire, telling my brother to "take a good look at her. This will be the last time that you can touch her and see her again," as I turned to walk out and handed Mom's outfit to the grievance counselor.

When I arrived at the car, I returned to the hotel and waited for my flight the next day. The next morning, I arrived at Phoenix Airport and was told Mom's remains would not be on that flight, leaving me in tears. Once I received my boarding passes, I called home to speak to my sister and explained my situation. It would leave me upset and unable to escape the tears falling from my eyes. It would not be long before my sister would say, "Don't worry. I will go to the airport and escort her to the funeral home," leaving me hurt, learning on that day I'd be bringing her remains home on Valentine's Day.

When Mom's remains arrived at midnight. I trusted my older sister to be there, escorting her remains to the funeral home, and I didn't call. Instead, I showered and gave Mark his medicine, lying at his feet and falling asleep. In the morning, I awakened, starting my day as normal as possible. When my assistant arrived at work, I went upstairs looking for music to take to the funeral for her wake. Thinking what she would love to hear, I came across some CDs that were purchased weeks before her death. When I placed the first CD that had "Regresa a Mi" (Unbreak My Heart), I was deeply moved by the words as tears invaded my eyes, being serenaded by Il Divo men. The song not only crept within the deeper part of my body, it would also bring back the pain of not staying longer speaking with Mom the last time I spoke to her.

Lying there, wishing I had another chance to speak to her again, I felt broken after hearing the song "Mama," shattering me into pieces. After hearing the next song "My Way," I felt she was with me, saying, "I made it over the mountain my way, crossing over the mountain to heaven." Although I wasn't a religious person. I realized she lived the remainder of her life on her terms, leaving my brother and sisters without any closure, although I was faced with many waves of trials. The one thing that left me wondering, with all the love she'd shown to my siblings, I never thought she would ever count on me for something. She needed me somehow; my life and family were more important, leaving me in tears and missing her even more.

That afternoon, after leaving the music at the funeral home. I knew my older brother and sister would arrive later that evening to spend time with Mom. I left them alone.

On the day of her wake, people arrived, and I saw my older sister sitting with her friends, who arrived with her, while I kept staring at the pictures that the funeral home had been playing, listening to the music. I remembered a mother who provided as much as she could. The one lesson I saw her do was she never gave up. She dealt with the struggles she faced as a mother. What you didn't know is, at one time, we were homeless and received clothes from organizations and living in the projects. My sister and I were provided food to eat for breakfast and lunch during the summer.

Living in the projects didn't make me feel embarrassed but taught me to appreciate having to go to a place with a roof above me and my siblings, knowing Mom was showing us a way of life as she remained strong throughout her struggles. Although Mom had a thyroid condition that caused her to gain weight, that didn't stop her in giving back, helping in the church or other agencies and organizations, giving back the things we received in our childhood years. When the viewing was over, I returned home, placing Mark to bed and sitting on the couch.

There I took some time rethinking about my younger years with Mom and my siblings, then I began to cry, recapping the hours of today, before showering and checking on Mark then falling asleep on the couch.

On the day of Mom's funeral, I would be arriving with my sons and daughter-in-law at the funeral home. I would see my older sister with some ladies arriving with her.

When the service began, Mom's pastor began to enlighten us about his conversation with Mom. He began by saying he spoke to Rita just days before her death. Rita called asking him; she wanted him to conduct her eulogy. When asked, he said he didn't believe Rita was going to pass away until he received a call from her daughter and was stunned hearing about her death.

"Your mother has done so many things for the church and helped out. Whenever she was needed, she was there. She is now at rest, and her labor has ended."

As I listened to every word her pastor was saying, I was wondering, *Why didn't she contact me sooner to say goodbye? But maybe she did when she mentioned to me about the mountains. She glanced at me. She was informing me she was going to make her last walk over the mountains without using a wheelchair or cane to the other side.* My mother was on her way out to the other side, where her heart and eyes were placed.

Once the pastor was finished speaking, I got up and spoke. I don't remember anything I said; however, the only thing I remember was those few minutes they were hovering over her casket, which was closed, sharing my last words "I love you," placing my head on her coffin, weeping. As soon as they brought her casket to the hearse, I was right behind her as they took her to her resting place. At the same time, my sister and her friends and my brother and his family made their way.

When the hearse stopped, I wouldn't be far from the car where Mark stayed sleeping as I watched them take Mom's body out of the hearse.

After my son and daughter-in-law got out of the car, I would be searching to see where my sister was at, and I would see her standing next to her friends. It was not long when the pastor prayed and blessed her coffin that I looked at Coco, telling him it was time to go, as the funeral employees waited for me to leave so I would not see Mom going to her resting place. After the funeral, I kept in touch with my half sister and became closer. Shortly after that, I became the executor to her estate, leaving Mom's divorce attorney to help me with what was needed to be done. Once Mom's lawyer finished up the paperwork of her estate and her things were divided between us, that would be the last time I would see my older brother and sister or know whatever is happening to my little brother, whatever they are doing with their life. One thing is for sure: I hope they are in good health, have peace, and found happiness from that day on.

The following weeks of searching for another doctor for Mark, I eventually find a doctor on the website and made him an appointment. I went to visit to speak with Dr. A, asking him to release Mark from his care to the neurologist I had found to treat Mark.

After handing Dr. A a letter, thanking him for helping me get Mark well, I returned home and faced an allegation and would see a case worker for Department of Human Services. That case would be closed many months later, and I would receive an apology from the case worker on the case and be told the school reported it. Though Dr. A and I thought she was delusional, I was grateful that the school was caught in the web of their lies. And if there was another case of Mark, they had a record of it.

Although the school didn't feel they were responsible for Mark's health with all the fall they noted on the report, it would be weeks later when I sit on the rocking chair when suddenly I would see feathers come falling above me. Getting up, I collected them and began to see the most beautiful pinkish color I had ever seen. I can't remember if I showed them to my neighbor or told her about that afternoon. However, she still remembers that day.

A few days later, I became stressed and overwhelmed. It was a late day in the evening when Israel called form Iraq to check on us. I was crying, missing Mom and feeling terrible not seeing Mark getting any better. Distressed, I was in tears talking to Israel about how I was feeling as he did his best to try to convinced me to stay strong. While we were talking, I began feeling a burning sensation in my arms. Asking Israel to hold on, I rose from the couch. Turning on the lights, I saw a welt of a cross on my wrist. At that moment, I ran upstairs, knocking on the bedroom door of Coco, showing him and my daughter-in-law, asking them to verify what this welted cross on my wrist I was seeing; before running downstairs, grabbing a disposable camera that I saw in the drawer and began taking pictures before getting back on the telephone, telling Israel about the strange thing that just happened.

The following morning, I went to take the disposable camera to have the film developed. After the children went home, I went to bring dinner home, stopping to pick up the pictures from the photo shop. After looking at the pictures, it was strange why I wouldn't be seeing the welt on any of the photos. Although I know what I saw and shown it to my son and daughter-in-law, somehow the wonder weighted heavily that it wasn't long when I called a good friend of mine, telling her my story about that account. Once she heard that account, she said that we shouldn't have any images or idols. "He had given you a spiritual cross, which no one but you and him knows. He gave you hope in the cross. You were given supernatural mark by God, remember that."

Listening to her strange response, it wouldn't be long when many more unbelievable things happened. My assistant and I would have no explanation, knowing I would not be alone in my trials.

If God was leading me to another direction in life, it made me wonder why since I wasn't a member of a church or religious organization.

Later in the week, I was back thinking about the welt of the cross as I sat uneducated about God, wondering what it all meant for me when suddenly I heard a knock on the door and saw two women standing. One of the women was named Mary and the other I couldn't recall. They were in the neighborhood and were Jehovah's Witnesses. There I was given a magazine before they read a scripture to me. After hearing them talk about God, I had many questions to ask and wanted answers when Mary said to me, she would come by later that week to talk.

In the coming week, Mark had a VNS implant while I waited to meet Dr. S. On the day of Mark's appointment, I arrived early at the appointment, hoping to find relief. When Dr. S examined Mark, his medication was reviewed, and some were changed to a lower dose and taken off and replaced with another kind of medicine. Within a week, I saw Mark awake, healthy, and improving. The treatment that Dr. S was doing brought tears to my eyes. Although Mark wouldn't be the same kid like he was before, I was excited to know I had a doctor to help me get Mark back to his feet, leaving relief in my heart.

Mark had everything he needed. He was given a home-bound teacher named Mr. Justice. At the same time, Mark's health was gradually improving. His speech was slow and slurry. It would take time for his teacher to understand what he was saying or asking. Sometimes Mr. Justice would take notes. One day, when Mr. Justice came to the kitchen, he asked if we were religious and had a Bible. I asked why. I answered him no, and we didn't have a Bible, even though Mark was baptized as Catholic. He shared something to me about Mark. He explained to me that lately, Mark has been saying things and written them down, and how one day he substituted a computer class. On that day, he used the computer and begin searching what Mark was describing, finding it in the Bible.

Unsure of what he was talking about, I remembered the welt and the things that were happening, trying to make sense of it. If God was talking to him, that could be the explanation of why he knew the Bible. I couldn't explain why Mark knew things in the Bible than Mr. Justice. However, it made me seek out what was going on with Mark, knowing if this was real.

When the witness came knocking one afternoon, I smiled, letting them in, and I asked so many questions, while they looked for the answered in their Bible. I was intrigued, wanting to learn more about God's love and be given a small book to read, "Remaining in God's Love." From that day on, I would have many more Bible studies with Mary and another woman.

I was excited learning and searching on Google building knowledge to know more about his love and the love of Jesus as my journey in life was heading to a peaceful place. I was reading Exodus 20:4: "Thou shalt not make unto thee any graven images or any likeness of anything that is in heaven above, or that is in the earth beneath, or that is in the water under the world." After remembering my Christian friend, I thought about God, the great things he has done for Mark and me. When the time came for Israel to return from his second deployment in Iraq, Mark and I arrived at Fort Stewart a few weeks early, searching for an apartment.

When I drove Mark and myself to Fort Stewart, it was late in the night. Mark got up and hit the corner of the end table, and I see him bleeding, a wound on the side of his head. I rushed him to the emergency room, feeling horrible that I had fallen asleep. That early morning, he had a few stitches. We returned back to the room, falling asleep again with him next to me. In the morning, I got up right before Mark awakened, showering before giving him his meds.

Once Mark was awake and dressed and had taken his medicine, I drove by where he once lived and saw there were apartments available and drove to the rental agency. After filling out the paperwork, I left a deposit and asked the woman how long it would take to hear from her.

She said next week. I'll told her what had happen at the Travelodge last night and my son's condition and willing to take it as is. She didn't make any promises but said she would try.

The next day, I heard from the apartment agency, letting me know that my application was approved; however, it would take a couple of days for the apartment to be ready. Excited, I told the woman I'd take the apartment as it was. After telling me she was going to look at the apartment and call me later that day, I waited for the call. It was nearly five o'clock when my cell phone rang, noticing the apartment agency was calling. When I answered, I was told that I could pick up the keys in the morning if I would like.

After hanging up, I was excited, knowing Mark would be in a more prominent and comfortable place with less furniture. The following day, after checking out and picking up the keys at the rental agency, Mark had to be lie on the floor while I called the water and light agency, switching the bills to my name. I called the cable company and ordered service. It would be a couple of hours when I saw Mark asleep that I got up and walked to the storage unit that was just across the street and began removing boxes and a mattress.

When two lawn men saw me moving things from the unit, one of the men stopped, asking if I needed help. The other man came over and asked if I wanted help for the couch too, and they did not only be carry the couch, they brought over all the heavy furniture, placing they in the apartment.

I handed them money. I returned to the storage unit and removed the remainder of the boxes, leaving the unit empty. After going to the office of the storage unit, I told the management that it was empty. When she asked if I wanted to drive Israel's car out of storage, I said, "No, let Israel come and get it." I returned to the apartment, began to unpack the kitchen boxes, placing the things in the dishwasher before realizing I didn't have any soap.

After taking a shower, I locked the door, leaving Mark asleep while I drove to the commissary, buying food and the things we needed. Shortly after arriving, Mark would still be asleep. I began washing the pots and pans to cook dinner for Mark and myself before the night settled in and before falling asleep.

The next day, I began unpacking the things that were still in the boxes. After all the boxes were emptied and the only thing needed to be done was to put the beds together, the thought of Israel coming home and we would have more time together made me excited. Even though I was feeling great, what really made me happy was knowing Mark was with me, giving me a huge relief.

On the day of Israel's return to Stewart, I was told there wouldn't be a huge ceremony, and we would be reunited at the same place on the grounds of Cortell. When the buses arrived, I was there and driving Israel to the apartment he lived many years ago. After placing the clothes into the dryer,

Israel saw Mark sleeping on the mattress of his twin bed. He got out of his BDU, moving the headboard that was placed in the second room, putting it together before placing a television for Mark to watch cartoons.

When Mark and I returned home, Israel's company was deployed for a third tour to Iraq, while he was left behind due to one of his eyes' sights. While he was getting treated, Israel made arrangement for Mark and me to meet him in Puerto Rico for Christmas.

When Mark and I arrived in San Juan, Israel and his aunt will be waiting. That would be the first time Israel's family would see Mark's condition and be heartbroken. As time went by, seeing Mark's condition, I would see the fear in the eyes of some of them. That bothered me. As I remained strong through all of my struggles I had faced in the past, I made sure, wherever Israel planned to go that it was a good place where Mark could rest if needed and wouldn't be far from my sight.

At the same time Israel and his family are celebrating Christmas and Three Kings days, Mark and I would attend some of the events; however, most of my time would be wanting to remain at the mother -in-law home studying God word up on the mountains, where I called paradise.

Later, when it came for Mark and me to return home, Israel brought his aunt with us to accompany him back to San Germán. When Mark and I arrived back home, I returned to work, while Mark returned to his homebound classes. Mark was doing a lot better and slowly returned to being himself. He was able to walk again and speak better than he did many months before. Although I wouldn't allow him alone in the shower or restroom, there were times that he would tell me, "Mom, I got it," and I would be grinding my teeth, fearing something would happen.

It took many more months when Mark made a full recovery. However, the cuts and abrasions would always remind about the past, when he was so sick. Mark would be needing care for the rest of his life and medicine to control his epilepsy. The thoughts of Mark being on medication the rest of his life would bother me, and I believe it did help Mark getting healed, but something inside me believed it was something more than medicine that guided his life back to where he has come back to being himself. I can't explain it, but what he was saying, I believed in my heart, is that God wasn't far from us. There are many stories that happened that will stay hidden between the *Lord* and me.

Going out to field ministry was one thing I loved doing. Sharing the news to the neighbor about Jehovah was something I never though one day I would be doing. However, many people seemed uninterested in the name Jehovah, which made me wonder why. Although they missed out something more imageable to believe, the blessing that transpired during that time.

Retirement

I t was in October 2010 when I returned to Stewart. This time, Israel was on leave for a few months before retiring after thirty-three years in the United States Army. When he arrived in San Antonio, I tried running my business at home; however, it be difficult to search for a location to move to. I was told that there was a day care facility and decided to go and talk to the person. When she said she was looking for a partner to help her purchase the building, I said it was not good to have partners when it comes to money, then I walked away.

Next, I went to the back where we got a loan to purchase another house and spoked to the loan officer, asking how could I obtain the name and address of the owner. She asked me for the address and would provide it to me. The next day, I wrote to the owner, informing her I was interested in renting her facility and when it would be available.

In late December, I got the keys to the facility, and my daughter-in-law would be the one clearing and cleaning while we slowly brought things over as we were getting all of our permits and inspections completed. Then I received a letter from the childcare licensing. That was the last certificate I needed, and I was excited. When she arrived in a heavy dress coat, she entered, and I met her at the door. She spoke, and I was confused of what she was asking. Leading her to the cafeteria, pointing out where was the huge tables that were there by the other owners. I stared at her, telling her I didn't know, forgetting what she was asking. She took off her coat and began her inspection. She went to every room and every shelf like a child, looking at the learning materials that were sitting there. When she came out of every room, everything was good but said we needed to add mirror in the infant and toddler room.

Once I saw her putting her coat on. The next thing I saw was her and her clipboard. She went to the children's playground to do an inspection. She would be out there for many minutes until the cold raced to her knees. I saw her coming back from inside. After several times of going in and out telling me how cold it was out there, she asked me to go outside with her and said some things had to be removed. Thinking about the thousands of dollars I paid for the commercial equipment, I asked her which ones I would move off the playground, when suddenly she asked me to help her move something around.

She was so sweet and determine to make things easier so she could take pictures. I thought she would be a great decorator one day. I was actually happy when I received my inspection. I had five things I needed to complete before receiving my license.

I received my initial licensed after Valentine's Day and my full licensed five months later. It would be three years later when the business did pick up. When the city project was competed and the bridge was opened, it was the week of Good Friday when I saw the barrels removed from the street. With a smile, I felt now I could get this building up and get a loan to own it. It took five years when that happened, but it wasn't easy. I was out knocking on doors, asking the neighborhood to sign a petition after hiring lawyer. It took two weeks. And with the help of one of my staff members, I applied for the both of us to become a notary, she would be the one stamping and, verifying the person and signatures before placing the signed document in the folder. There is a story of what happened on one of those day while we were sitting in the car. That summer, I was baptized as a Jehovah's Witness. That day I left the convention of the Jehovah's Witness being among thousands that were baptized, our lives working in the kingdom of God. Shortly after being baptized, I felt my face expanding and red as it was burning me, and I rushed to the hotel room into the shower. I didn't know what caused my face to burn the way it did, even though my friend and I were amazed how my face looked.

A few years later, I stop attending meetings, and there was a church by my home that I went to check out. On that Sunday morning, I was fired up with his sermon, and my heart was thrilled, wanting to hear more about his love for Jesus. I kept attending both services. By then I was singing in the choir. While I continued going to the Baptist Church, I always remained serving Jehovah. The congregation and the senior pastor didn't know I was a baptized Jehovah's Witness. And after my second time being a vacation Bible director, I informed them I was leaving the choir and wanted to return to field ministry.

After making that choice, my life became disarrayed, and I wondered what was happening. It took a few years of trying to get the things back to order as I kept saying to myself Jehovah loves me. If the trails I was facing was trying to destroy me, it might've hurt me deeply. There were more challenges coming my way that tried to destroy me.

A day came when I saw myself paralyzed, and I cried out to the Almighty God, telling him, "Don't let him do this to me. What about Mark? Who will care for him?" Tears fell from my face.

It began on a Sunday morning that I went back to the Baptist Church after writing more pages in my book. When I returned into my car, I saw small red polka dots above my hair line and hand, wondering what they were. After taking a nap, I woke up and saw more, wondering what they were. While I was trying to remember the last things I touched, I remembered holding a man's hand, as often do when we are gathering together in prayer. I tried to figure out what they could be. I told Israel I was going to the emergency room to seek answers to these mysterious sores. After being examined by the doctor, I was given a steroid shot and another medicine to help with the sores. The following day, I was at work, sitting on a desk chair. Pain started to rise, and I asked one of employees to hand me my bottle that was in the first-aid cabinet, they're taking the pill. It didn't make me feel better, so I went back to the emergency room to get reevaluated by another doctor. I was treated as having hand-foot-and-mouth disease. I was given a stronger steroid to take for a week, and by late Friday, I went to meet a friend for dinner. I was sitting and feeling worse, unable to arise and make my way to the car.

After arriving home, Israel was at the driveway, placing a small trash bag into the container. When he saw my condition I was in, he began to laugh, asking, "What's wrong with you?" which I didn't know. I walked slowly in the house. When I arrived upstairs, I got undressed and took the medicine the doctor prescribed me and climbed a chair to get on my bed and fell asleep. It was one o'clock in the morning when I awakened in pain, unsure what was happening to me. When I finally was able to get out of bed, I saw Mark sleeping. I made my way down the stairs and saw Israel sleeping. Unsure if I should wake him up to ask him to drive me to the hospital as I stood there in pain. Deciding I need him to care for Mark, I placed my identification neck chain around my neck, walked to the car, and drove off. How I was able to drive in my condition was a mystery; however, shortly after arriving, my whole limbs wouldn't be functioning. While I sat in triage, the doctors came in and out, asking questions and personal questions. The pain became more aggressive, and the doctors took pictures too, wondering what the sore was.

It took many hours before one of the doctors got concerned, telling me that my blood levels were so high, unsure what was causing it. Later that morning, I sat in a holding room until my room was ready. When I was brought to the ward, I was on my back as my eyes and head were the only thing I was able to move. When a nurse returned to my room, she introduced herself and told me about the services and the persons who would be taking care of me. After listening to her, I was asked, if I would want to be resuscitated. Lying there, I was wondering why she asking me this, thinking I'd be back on my feet once they had given me the correct medication. She kept staring at me like she needed an answer, thinking her question was a joke. I looked at her, replying, "No, just let me die." After I gave her my answer, she stormed out quickly, and she came back with the doctor who was in charge of my care.

When I saw them came closer to me, he asked if it was okay that he sit in the chair that was next to me. He said, "Look, you don't know how sick you are. All we need is your tongue to swell, cutting off air, and you die. You need to remember, you're too young for this to happen." They both stared at me, waiting for my answer. I told the nurse it would be okay for them to resuscitate me if needed. Once the doctor and the nurse walked out of the room, I looked up toward the heaven, crying, telling, "Jehovah, don't let him (Satan) do this to me." I knew I was being tested, and I would accept whatever happens but also knew he would come and rescue me. No sooner after saying this, I fell asleep. When I awakened, I heard noises and saw a housekeeper preparing the bed across from me. When she grabbed hold of the curtains and pushed them all the way back, I closed my eyes falling back to sleep.

Hours later, I was awakened, hearing two men talking in the dark room. Looking at where the voices were coming from, I couldn't see anyone. I felt uncomfortable, wondering what to do. It was in those few minutes, as I stayed listen to them speaking, when I began to whisper, "Hello." After doing so, the room became still and the only noise I heard was the ponding sound of my heart as anxiety overwhelmed me, unable to move.

Shortly after my first whisper, I whispered again, leaving me in fear as I shut my eyes and fell back to sleep. After I was back to sleep, I was awakened again for the third time, feeling as if someone was kicking my bed while hearing rapid sounds of ticking. I panicked, jumping up and pressing on the nurse button. When I heard a woman voice on the intercom, I went hysterical, asking her to come. Something strange was happening in my room.

When the light in the room were turned on, I saw two nurses coming toward me and began pressing on the control panel, trying to get the ticking sound to stop. After several attempts, the woman nurse stopped and watched the other nurse, who kept pressing on the buttons. She notices what they were doing wasn't working. She asked the male nurse to help her move the hospital bed forward to unplug the cord from the wall before plugging it back in. After doing several times, he stood, hearing the woman nurse telling him to drop the power cord as she reexamined my care plan. I was moved to "bed one" and was covered up, asking if there was anything more I needed. After telling her no, the lights in my room went off, and I was in the dark again, falling back to sleep before noticing it was 3:23 in the morning.

When the sun rose that Sunday morning, I awakened with all functions of my limbs. I rose and hurried to the shower to get washed up. You couldn't imagine the feeling I had seeing myself back on my feet. The thoughts of ever walking again weighed heavy on my mind. That terrified me. However, I knew, no matter how the feeling that I had controlled me, there was no doubt in mind the power of God's love wasn't far from my hand.

After showering and ordering breakfast, I saw my doctor noticing I was up and walking around, which surprised him! The expression on his face said it all. In disbelief, he asked me, "What did the nurses give you?"

I replied, "You don't know." Blood thinners came to mind, which I told him. Smiling, he took another look at me. I asked if I could go home, he replied no, looking dumbfounded by my recovery. The thoughts of my limbs functioning again brought tears to my eyes. If my answered was bizarre, I couldn't imagine how he would react if I shared with him what occurred in the wee morning hour. Although I knew it had a lot to do with my recovery, it brought relief in trusting something you can't see or understand.

I was discharged late Monday evening. I had many more labs and tests to be completed. I sat in the waiting room at the rheumatologist office. Later, when all the test and examinations were competed, the doctor wouldn't find the reasons what caused my body to shut down. They knew my immune system was being attacked but had no explanation why. Although I was diagnosed with an autoimmune deficiency, I went back and began thinking when the blisters started and realized it began when I returned back to writing my story, leaving me worried what would happened next.

It was a sunny day on a Saturday afternoon in 2018. Israel just arrived home from the gym, right at the time when I was about to drive off to the grocery, shopping for the day care. When Israel got out of his car, I got off the car to talk to him, asking what he wanted me to bring home for him to eat. Undecided, pizza came to mind, and I said to myself, "Mark likes pizza," telling him I was bringing back pizza. As drove off, I was feeling exhausted. As I drove to the pizza place, I ordered the pizza, taking it home. After getting out of my clothes and into my pajamas, I began listening to gospel music. I took off my headsets and began eating a slice of pizza. I heard a loud squealing sound coming from the hallway. When I got up and looked, all I saw was Mark's hands dropping down. I raced to his room, calling out to him.

At the same time I was calling him, I saw he wasn't breathing, and I screamed for Israel to call 911. When he came upstairs, I heard him yelling, "Get off of him." I asked him to help me get him off the bed to do CPR. When I saw Israel not listening to my instructions, I grabbed Mark's shirt, pulling him toward me. Suddenly I would hear him coughing back to life as I get off the bed. I went to the bathroom, looking for a towel. I saw myself drained in fear.

When I went back to the room, I told Israel to call 911, but he wouldn't listen, saying we would take him to the emergency room. He cleaned Mark, and I rushed getting into clothes. I drove in front, while he stayed behind me. I was grateful, praying, thanking God I was there when this happened to Mark. Unsure what was wrong with Mark, I kept my eyes on the rearview mirror. I saw him dropping his head, leaving me frightened as I hurried to get to the hospital. When we arrived at the emergency room, Mark was rushed to triage, where I would hear a doctor's voice telling the nurse to give him a shot and another before he went into the room, letting me know that he contacted neurology and was going to admitted Mark into the hospital. When the doctors of neurology arrived, they asked who was treating Mark and what happened that caused us to bring him to the emergency room. There I was, reliving the fear I the pain that I had experienced. After she was giving every detail that happened, she began to examine Mark. Looking at his hands and feet and body, she came around me and raised Mark's eyes. I saw his eyes rolled back, unsure why. The neurologist left to speak to the doctor who was caring for Mark. I stared at the doctor. I told Israel to get up and go home and bring clothes for me and Mark. Once Israel left the hospital, the doctor returned to Mark's room and asked me to follow him. I was taken to a waiting room, where he told me that Mark was going to be placed in life support. The doctor showed me where I would wait until he came and got me. While we were heading back to where Mark was. I saw nurses and other professionals going to where Mark was. Suddenly, the doctor stopped asking for me to return to the room that he showed me to wait. As I sat in that room for a few minutes, I prayed silently, fearing what I would see when I go back to the room. As tears rolled down my face, I went outside and called one of friends, telling her what was happening. When she heard what was happening to Mark, she told me she was on her way to the emergency hospital where Mark was being treated. After hanging up with her, I called my son Coco, asking him to go to the house and wait for Dad and return back with him.

Asking what was happening, I told Coco that Mark was sick and was going to be placed on life support, and I didn't want his dad to be alone without support when he returned to the hospital. When I called my sister last, I would learn she was out of town and couldn't come but would be back home tomorrow. After calling my son, my friend, and my sister, I continued praying, calling on Jehovah, unsure what was next for Mark. I went back to the waiting room. I just got seated when I saw the doctor standing on the threshold, calling me over, telling me, "It's remarkable. Your son is awake and is calling for you." I felt lifted in high spirits, thanking Jehovah, seeing Mark gleaning from ear to ear before hearing one of the nurses saying this was a miracle. Leaving me engulfed in happiness, praising God for what he had done in front of a group of professionals.

When Mark was taken to the ICU ward, I remained with him. When we were alone, I got myself comfortable, calling Israel, remembering I wanted to attend church to sing on the choir. I wanted to share all the happiness I was feeling with my friends of the congregation. Although many didn't know anything about I wouldn't tell anyone that my son was in the hospital except one. After my sister in choir followed me to my home and I got changed, she followed me to the hospital and met Mark and Israel. When the time came for my friend from church to leave, Israel was ready to leave too. I told Israel I needed him here at five o'clock in the morning to stay with Mark. He said goodbye, while Mark cracked, laughing.

As I got my bed ready, which was a chair, I see that Mark went to sleep. I went to sleep too and awaken early the next day. The following morning, I waited for Israel. The time was past five o'clock. I called Israel, waking him up, telling him I was leaving for work. I told the nurse my husband was going to be here soon. He told me not to worry; he would keep an eye on Mark.

Afterward, as I arrived at work, I sat on my desk in the classroom when my cell phone lit up. When I answered it, I heard Israel's voice telling me he slipped in the tub and thought he had broken some of his ribs. Unsure about his condition, I called most of the morning; he wouldn't answer. It wouldn't be long that I contacted Coco, asking if he could go check on his brother and father, who were at the same hospital. After calling Coco several times, I drove to the hospital to check on Mark. Mark's nurse told me that Israel could not withstand the pain and could not wait so he went to the emergency room to be seen. When the nurse checked and saw that Israel was still being treated in the emergency room, I went over and saw Coco waiting in the foyer in the waiting room. As I was taken to triage, I saw Israel hooked up with oxygen. There I sat, noticing the doctors that were there on Saturday were working again and now treating my husband. I sank into my chair, doing my best for them not to recognize me. While I remain seated, I was wondering what are the chances of this happening to another family member. As I sat there, it seemed like something you would be watching on true crime detectives, and there Israel told me he was being admitted also to another ICU in a different area where Mark was.

When I was ready to leave, I left Coco to watch over Mark and Israel, and I returned to work. There I prayed to Jehovah, asking for his help. Later, after I closed the day care facility. I drove back to the hospital to check up on Mark and was told he would be discharged. After I collected his and my things, I receive Mark's discharge papers and wheeled him to the ICU, where his father was being taken care. When Coco pressed the button, we were told it would be an hour until we would able to see him. It wouldn't be long when I made up my mind, taking Mark to the car, driving him home. When we arrived home, I took Mark to his bed to lay him down before letting the dog Chu-chu out. It was there as I was standing that I looked around and saw a huge wall of mist standing in front of the bushes. I was wondering why it was there, then I took my eyes away from it, walking to call Chu-chu back. I wouldn't see it there.

I was told that Israel had broken three ribs and would stay in the hospital for a while. After having an outpatient operation to remove a tumor on his tongue weeks before, now he was in the hospital. He remained in ICU, and the doctor performed a procedure that Israel knew about, leaving me unaware. When Israel was released from the hospital, he would be healing. It took a few days later when I was eating with a few of my staff when he called me. He asked if I could take him to a procedure he would be having. I wondered what the procedure would be. His voice became weak when I heard him say cancer. At that moment, I asked, "What do you mean you have cancer? How long did you know about this?"

As I listened to Israel's explanation, I was told that recently, during his stay in the hospital, a biopsy was taken, and it was found out that he had stage two cancer, leaving me upset that Israel had never mentioned it to me. I began crying while my staff watched.

After I hung up, I became emotional and started to cry. Here we went again; I was falling apart. my staff comforted me, and the lunch we had bought got cold as we sat in disappoint, seeing me in tears. As we were sitting, we heard in the room a bang on the widow, leaving us scared. One crawled on the floor toward the door. I was frozen. I asked my staff who was behind me. When one of them looked out the window and did not see anyone, I got up and looked too before returning to sit and sit and talk when suddenly we heard the entrance door opened. When we looked out of the window and didn't see a car parked out in front, we were scared again. That day would be one of many things that happened there that we couldn't explained. Though all the unexplained things began many years before when I opened up my center.

Somehow, what was happening at the facility or home was something I couldn't explained. I knew who had the power to get me through, and I continued praising and worshipping, never forgetting who brought me back to my feet. If I was being protected by his grace, I had many stories to talk about. Although I left many bizarre, unexplained stories hidden within me.

The day came for Israel to have the procedure for the pin to be placed to begin his chemo immediately. I was by his side, listening to his doctor and was told he was on stage two Hodgkin's lymphoma. That afternoon, we returned home, and I went to my computer and sang to the *Lord*. I knew I needed him. At the time, worry crowded my mind as tears dropped from my eyes. I knew I had to deal with what was to come as I kept reminding Israel to stop saying he was going to die, crushing me inside. The following day, after closing the facility Israel called, letting me know he was going to pick up dinner for Mark, and I would meet up with him. There he handed Mark's food to me before showing me a document of his last will and testament that he picked up from a law firm. It was there that I looked at him, asking, "Don't do this to me," grabbing Mark's food as tears flooded out of my eyes. When I returned home, I gave Mark his medicine before escaping to prayer and worship. I knew, if I was going to get through my hurt and pain, I needed something much greater than my own strength.

When Israel completed his first cycle of chemo, it left him weak, leaving me upset why he didn't try eating something to regain his strength. It was at that moment that I had to say something.

"You're not dead. Stop letting me see you're giving up."

When I saw the poignancy in his eyes, my heart dropped. I turned away, feeling his hopelessness. Nevertheless, I remained close to God Almighty, trusting he would bring Israel from his darkened moments. Meanwhile, while Israel didn't have an appetited to eat. I would drive and support his next cycle of chemo.

The day before that Wednesday, before Israel began his second cycle of chemo, I arrived home that evening and cooked fish and vegetables for Israel and made Mark a hamburger with fries. At the same time I was cleaning up the kitchen, I noticed I didn't make anything for me to eat. Just as I was cleaning up and moving the microwave, I found a small bag of brownies behind it, smiling. After cleaning up the kitchen, I looked at the clock and noticed I had a half hour before meeting my hairstylist and friend at her home to cut and dye my hair. While I waited for the time to come, I was standing, looking out the kitchen window, speaking to God before opening the cabinet for a glass to pour me some milk. It was just a matter of minutes after placing the first brownie in my mouth with a dip of milk that I froze. The banging came from the corner of the window. I tiptoed to the bedroom, telling Israel what just happened. He said he heard the sound, thinking I was chopping something. I replied no, I was staring out of the window before telling him goodbye, that I would be back.

When I arrived at my friend's house, I took my glasses and the last three brownies that were still in the bag. I wanted to recap and demonstrate what happened in the kitchen with the glass of milk and brownies, but she be running late, and I sipped on my milk and ate my brownies until she arrived.

During the weeks when Israel was on his second cycle in the spring 2019. he was on his second treatment when something horrible happened. It was a weekday after returning home from work. I saw Israel on the side of the bed.

He told me he wasn't feeling well. I asked why he didn't call me. He said he didn't want to worry me, so he waited until I got home. I asked him if he had eaten. He said no, that he had a hard time breathing. After hearing he had a difficult time breathing, I told Israel to call his doctor, letting him know I was taking him to the emergency room. After showering, I took Israel to the car and drove off. When I arrived at the emergency room, I left my car in the front entrance of the emergency room and wheeled him in.

When the nurse began to do vitals, I told her I needed to move my car, leaving Israel's care with her. Minutes later, after retuning, I saw the nurse talking to Israel, unsure what was happening. Suddenly she raises her voice, calling for help, telling the other nurse to get him to triage and give him oxygen. When we arrived in the nurses' station and Israel was placed in a huge room, I saw the nurse placing a tube in his nose before cutting his shirt to place cables to monitor him. Israel's oxygen was really low, and the X-ray showed he had double phenomena. The doctors observed Israel's oxygen level was low. It was three o'clock in the morning when I returned home to gather personal items Israel wanted and gave Mark his medication.

When the staff came back to work, I went to the hospital, which wasn't far from my workplace, and saw Israel trying to beat the fear that was overpowering him. I knew, at that moment, I had to convince myself that the *Lord* would bring him out of his darkest moments but also knew Israel had to believe it for himself, asking God Almighty to change his situation, which I knew that it was something hard for him to do. So with that, I became Israel's advocate, asking, "*God*, my God Jehovah, you never failed me now," and continued worshipping and praising Jehovah, knowing he has been good to me. Israel would be in the hospital for many weeks, while I was caring for Mark and the dog and running my business. I was exhausted and had little strength. I sought the *Lord* with praise and prayer. After closing the center one evening, after feeding Mark, I returned to the hospital to see Israel.

Upon my arrival, I met the team of doctors who were looking over Israel's care and was told about the complications Israel had early in the morning, making adjustment to his plan of care. Bothered why Israel didn't mention this to me, I played it off, smiling happily that he was alive. Although Israel was closed to being placed on life support, they placed him on another oxygen machine. Israel was complaining; he liked the other one. Israel would have a few friends of his come to visit and pray for him. Although I felt joy in my heart seeing his friends praying with him, I was praying that he opened up his heart and eyes to the *Lord* and seek him.

It was in the middle of the week when one of Israel's doctors called me. She began telling me that she had spoken to Israel and given him a list of rehabilitation centers for him to go.

I asked when Israel would begin his chemo. She instantly said no to chemo, that it would kill Israel. Fighting back tears, I replied, "What do you mean you're not going to begin treating his cancer?" When I listened to her, I asked if they could at least check to see if the cancer changed in his system. She answered with a no. She said, "I know how you feel before grabbing the phone harder and slamming it into the desk, hanging up."

She didn't know how I was feeling or what I was thinking, what was happening in my life. A little later, another doctor contacted me regarding Israel about finding him a treatment center. When I went to see Israel that night in the hospital, he gave me the brochure that the doctor had given him to give to me, leaving the hospital that night before coming against a storm.

Yes, after leaving Israel hospital, lightening was flashing. Suddenly, the rain and wind became violent, and I was yelling and crying, saying over and over, "Let your Kingdom come. Let your will be done." I saw the car's blinker blinking as lightning flashed across the skies. I remained focus, steadfast, repeating, "Let your kingdom come and will be done." When I arrived home, I ran into the house soaked, hearing the thunder before the lights went off. Looking out of the door in the kitchen, I saw Israel's bird's cage moving by the impact of the wind. After calling Israel that his bird cage might fall, he told me to bring it in, and I said no. The weather was worse to return outside.

The next morning. I returned early at work. One of the children's parents talked about the storm. He said, "I live many years in Florida and never experienced a storm of that magnitude." Although I knew I was battling something, I didn't know what. At the same time, I was caring for Mark and Israel. I prayed to the *Lord* to watch over Coco, believing he would and could be next. If the devil tried to stop me and didn't get far and got Mark and didn't get far, I felt the power of darkness was coming to take him out, and I wasn't going to let that happened.

It would be a few days later when I found a place for Israel to receive care. Knowing that the emergency room was on the property made me less worried. On that Saturday afternoon, the hospital sent their EMS to pick Israel from the hospital, bringing him to their facility. When Israel arrived, his room would be across of the nurses' station. He was given a seven-day schedule before being discharged home. At that moment, Israel believed He needed more than seven days to get better and walk. When the seven days came the following week, he was walking and his health improving. At the same time, I was driving Israel to his doctor's appointment. One of his appointments would make me blush. It was when Israel's name was called by the doctor. When Israel got up, the doctor saw my hand on the wheelchair, saying, "Where are you going with that?" asking me to leave the wheelchair behind. I grabbed Israel's oxygen tank and placed it over my shoulder. When we arrived in his office, he went over Israel's medical records and called him by his rank when Israel began, in respect, asking him to call him by his name as he began to laugh.

Hearing Israel's doctor discussing that throughout all the years he's been a physician, he would be the only patient surviving everything his patients couldn't. When Israel began explaining to the doctor the struggles he had to endure, my heart would be thanking and praising Jehovah that Israel would celebrate his birthday in November 2019 and the following year, in April 2020, after Israel gets his CT scan, it would show no cancer in his system, leaving me excited, trying not to cry.

By the summer, I heard about COVID as the government kept all childcare centers updated, not knowing what lies ahead. Although we remained open, our students and their families remained home.

Two years later, the staff and I were infected by the virus. They were taking precautions. I reserved a hotel room for nine days. But what happened on Sunday morning kept me on my feet. I awakened, hearing someone preaching a sermon. I saw a preacher saying over and over, "Be strong and courageous. Have I not commanded you? Be strong and courageous. Do not be afraid. Do not be discouraged, for the Lord, your God, will be with you wherever you go."

At that moment, I began crying, remembering everything I went through, feeling as if he was there talking to me when I immediately grabbed my cell phone and began recording what was happening. After recording some of the sermons, I ran to the shower and made myself oatmeal, turning the television on in the living room and hearing the same speech at the exact time I was recording twenty minutes earlier: "Stay strong and courageous, and do not be discouraged, for the Lord, your God, will be with you wherever you go."

That wasn't all of it. It would be many months later when I had emergency surgery. I returned to the emergency room, dehydrated and exhausted. Once I was examined, the doctor returned to speak with me and was told I needed to go back into the operating room.

I had fluid in my stomach, and it needed to be removed. As I waited for the doctors to perform the surgery early in the wee morning hours, I prayed, knowing that if I returned to the operating table, I wouldn't be able to survive the surgery. When the doctors arrived at the hospital and came to see me, I was told they would look at the scan and return shortly. After the doctors left me alone, I began to pray. I suddenly heard and saw the paper towel container rolling a paper towel sheet from its devise and knew that the *Lord* was here with me. I waited for the doctors to return. It will not be long before the nurse arrived, saying, "You're going home." Hearing that I was going home brought music to my ears, leaving me excited.

Once I arrived home early that morning, I noticed I had two hours left before returning to work. After drifting to

sleep, I felt my body burning and began sweating off whatever it was leaving my clothes wet.

Somehow, while remembering everything I suffered and
what my family went through, there would never be a day I
didn't tell someone at work about his greatness and love for
me. Many years later, Dr. S would be retiring, and I would
search for another great doctor and found one, seventy-seven
miles away in Austin. He got Mark back to nearly having
any seizures. The trial medicine drug that Mark was taking
was helping him and feeling it was a gift from heaven. I was
seeing a dramatic change in Mark's health. However, there is
a story behind this account. I didn't want to share the stories,
but I wanted it to remain in my heart as a mother. This wasn't
about me, Mark, and Israel. It was about a loving God who
delivered me from many challenges I never thought I would
face.

At the same time, Mark is getting well. It wouldn't be
long after I saw Israel sick again when he heard the doctor
telling him he had fluid around his heart. The doctor gave
him three options: If he didn't have the surgery, he could
get an infection and die, or they could accidentally poke his
heart and die. The third possibility is the fluid getting into his
heart and killing him. After the doctors warned Israel of the
options, the surgeons refused the surgery and told him they
would monitor his health. Smiling, I knew Jehovah would
have a plan for Israel, waiting within that week. So when
Israel told me his doctor would do the surgery. I knew it was
going to be a success; however, it wouldn't be long when the
fluid reappeared again, leaving Israel no choice but to return
to the operating room, where the doctor would make a window in his chest, for the fluid could leak when Israel was
discharged from the hospital. He was back home and on his
feet with another thirty days of antibiotics.

I saw everything around me was returning to normal. I held on to my devotion to Jehovah in worship and prayers. I remembered the battles I had to fight. Although they seemed very hard to withstand, somehow I'll learned it's okay to fear if you choose to give up. But whatever it was, it didn't allow me to give up, learning to resist whatever came my way. I knew who held my yesterday, today, and tomorrow. Now that my heart and mind are leading me to the kingdom of God, would I be ready for my next chapter?

The answer to that question would be an almighty yes, I would be ready because the calling isn't from a church; it was given from above and the experience that transformed me and prepared me for this day. I knew the risk Jesus and the disciples had on their lives. The goal would be the same; we come in bringing the *good news*, like what is written in Psalm 91 and forever written.

He that dwell in the secret place of the most high shall abide under the shadow of the Almighty. I will say to the Lord; he is my refuge and my fortress: my God, in him will I trust.

Indeed, he will deliver thee from the snare of the fowler and the noisome pestilence. He shall cover thee with his feather and under his wings shalt thou trust his trust shall be thy shield and buckler, thou shall not be afraid for the terror night; nor for the arrow that flieth by day;

Because he hath set his love upon me, therefore will I deliver him: I will set him on high because he hath my name, he shall call on my name, and I

will answer him: I will be with him in
trouble; I will deliver him and honor him
with long life will I satisfy him, and shew
him my salvation.

I was totally convinced who I was and where I had to be.
I ensured I completed my second goal of receiving my degree
before taking the summer off to spend time with Mark and
Israel in Puerto Rico. There I would be spending time with
Israel's family. I began finishing my third goal after completing the manuscript. By the end of July, I would spend time
with my sons, grandsons, and friends on Padre Island, resting
for my next chapter. However, my manuscript will have an
ending. Although my work for the kingdom would begin
shortly after returning to the prayer house, at the same time,
I am preparing for my next chapter, excited about what it
will bring.

The End

About the Author

Debra A. Martinez is a business owner and a pre-kindergarten teacher. Debra lives in San Antonio, Texas, with her retired sergeant major husband Israel, her oldest son Israel III, and Mark where she continues preaching the assignment God Almighty leads her to do. She thought she had everything in control while her husband was deployed in Iraq, but nothing would prepare her for what will happen next…

www.underhisshadow.site

Printed in the USA
CPSIA information can be obtained
at www.ICGtesting.com
CBHW032033011024
15215CB00056B/1923